BALANCED SUCCESS

LEAD YOURSELF. ALIGN YOUR LIFE.
THRIVE IN THE AGE OF DISRUPTION.

TANYA MILLS

First published in 2025 by Aligned Success
© Tanya Mills 2025
The moral rights of the author have been asserted
All rights reserved. Except as permitted under the Australian Copyright Act 1968 (for example, a fair dealing for the purposes of study, research, criticism or review), no part of this book may be reproduced, stored in a retrieval system, communicated or transmitted in any form or by any means without prior written permission.
All inquiries should be made to the author.

ISBN: 978-1-7643362-0-8

Printed in Australia
Internal icons and illustrations designed by
Alysha Anema: alysha@anemadesigns.com - anemadesigns.com
Interior layout and book cover design by
David Schembri Studios: dschembristudios@gmail.com - davidschembristudios.com
Editing by Tania Hudson

Disclaimer
The material in this publication is of the nature of general comment only, and does not represent professional advice. It is not intended to provide specific guidance for particular circumstances and it should not be relied on as the basis for any decision to take action or not take action on any matter which it covers. Readers should obtain professional advice where appropriate, before making any such decision. To the maximum extent permitted by law, the author and publisher disclaim all responsibility and liability to any person, arising directly or indirectly from any person taking or not taking action based on the information in this publication.

For Judy & Steve

CONTENTS

Introduction: 7

Rebuilding Your Idea of Success

Chapter One 13
A Wake-up Call to Realign

Chapter Two 23
Born to Win, Wired to Perform

Chapter Three 31

Creating the Destination and Upgrading the Plane

Chapter Four 39
Redefining Success

Chapter Five 49
Health & Vitality

Chapter Six 87
Mental Wealth

Chapter Seven 135
Growth and Contribution

Chapter Eight 145
Connection

Chapter Nine 153
Abundance & Finance

Chapter Ten 163
Fun, Joy & Creativity

Chapter Eleven 175
Business & Career

Chapter Twelve 183
Spiritual Alignment

Chapter Thirteen 191
Balanced Success Life – Taking Action

Chapter Fourteen 203
The Journey Ahead Lead With Conscious Courage

References 207

INTRODUCTION:

Rebuilding Your Idea of Success

Picture this.

You're sitting at your desk. It's 7:45 p.m. The office is quiet, the inbox is still full, and your to-do list has somehow grown since midday. You're tired, but you keep going. You tell yourself you'll slow down next week, after this deadline, after that project.

Sound familiar?

For many leaders, this is just life. The pace is constant. The demands never stop. And somewhere along the way, we start to believe this is normal; that success requires sacrifice, and being stretched thin is simply the cost of ambition.

But what if that version of success is quietly costing us more than we realise? This book is for everyone. It's for those who've ticked the boxes—career, business, responsibility, reputation—but still feel something is off. It's for those who know they're capable of more, but aren't sure what more really means anymore. It's for the people who look successful on the outside, but on the inside feel disconnected, scattered, or are quietly asking: Is this it?

If that's you, you're not alone, and you're not broken. You might just be misaligned. Misalignment occurs when our thoughts, choices and life systems are not in sync with our values. It's when our understanding of what constitutes success doesn't line up with our practices, and we start to question our sense of self and our self-worth.

And now, more than ever, we don't have the luxury of staying misaligned.

We are living through one of the most significant shifts in human history.

Artificial Intelligence is just one massive change. AI is not just changing how we work, it's changing how we live. How we connect, communicate, think, create, parent, learn, lead and make decisions. It's rewriting the pace and pattern of life itself. In just a few short years, the ground beneath us has begun to move faster than most of us know how to keep up with.

We're scrolling more, responding faster, adapting constantly. Many are thriving externally, yet internally are quietly drowning. What's being tested now isn't just business acumen or digital skills. What's being tested is our capacity to stay human.

In a world increasingly run by algorithms, automation and acceleration, the leaders who will thrive are not the busiest or most brilliant. They are the ones who are grounded. Self-aware. Aligned.

And by leaders, I mean leaders at every level. Leaders are not just CEOs or C-suite executives. They are not necessarily Department Heads or Head Coaches. Leaders can be found on hospital wards and in classrooms, in volunteer groups and in sporting teams. We are all leaders, and we all have a responsibility to those around us to show up as our best selves, knowing exactly who we are and what we stand for.

Because if we don't know who we are, we will be led by whatever is loudest, whether that's an algorithm, an inbox or a cultural current that doesn't reflect our values.

This book is an invitation to pause. To reflect. To rebuild a version of success that doesn't cost you your health, your peace or your purpose.

It blends insight, action and regular check-ins while asking you to look honestly at your definition of success and how it must change. So let me start by asking you this:

- How's your energy, *really*?
- When was the last time you felt fully present with the people you love?
- Are your choices aligned with your values, or with your calendar?
- Do you feel proud of the life you're building, or just busy inside it?

These aren't easy questions. But they are the ones that matter. Because the cost of ignoring them is living a life that looks good on the outside but feels hollow on the inside.

Through my story, you'll meet a version of me who looked like she had it all together, but was silently falling apart. From a childhood spent on the winning dais as a champion athlete, to a young adulthood marked by insecurity and a decade-long eating disorder, to becoming a grown woman running businesses on different continents…and running herself into the ground in the process, my own story is one of chronic misalignment.

Happily, in this book you will also meet the woman who emerged after doing the real work—not just to rebuild a business, but to reclaim a life that felt meaningful.

This book is part memoir, part guidebook and part call to action for a new kind of leadership. One that honours not just achievement, but alignment.

It's not a linear read. After the first few chapters, you're invited to follow what feels most relevant. Each chapter explores a different part of what I call the *Balanced Success Wheel*, a framework I created to help leaders realign with what matters.

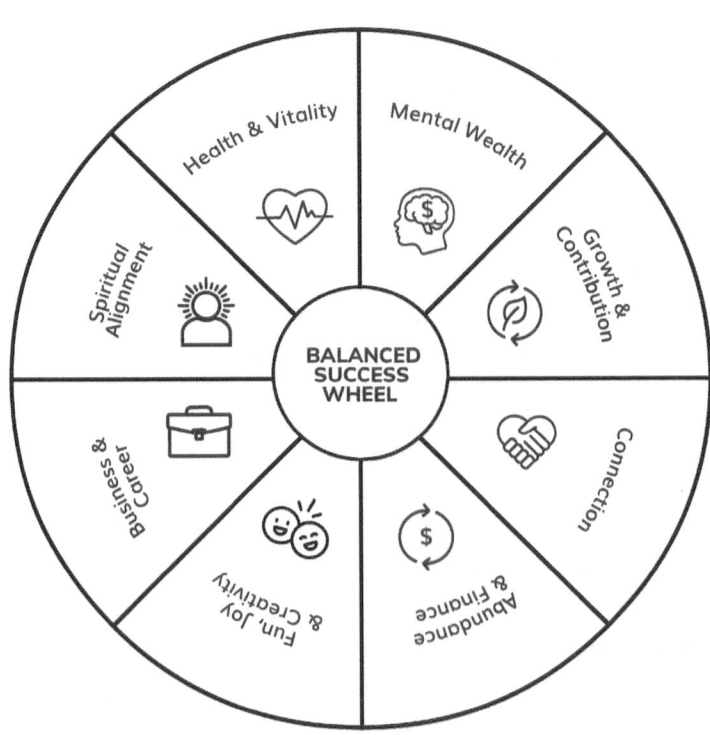

Start where you feel called. But eventually, come back to the parts you resist, because our blind spots often hold our biggest breakthroughs.

This isn't about easy answers. But it *is* about asking better questions. The kind that open doors. The kind that rewire futures.

Because the world doesn't need more burnt-out leaders.

It needs clear, connected ones.

It needs *you*.

I wrote this book because it is a resource I wish I'd had when my life was horribly misaligned, and I was teetering on the precipice of breaking down in more ways than one.

Join me on a journey to discover what true success really means, and to redefine your life from the inside out.

Tanya

CHAPTER ONE

A Wake-up Call to Realign

Life is busy and demanding. We live in a world that praises those who can juggle more, respond faster and stretch themselves thinner. Technology was meant to make life easier—a helping hand to free up space and create efficiency. But is it really helping? Or has it become another layer of noise, pushing us to solve more problems, move at a faster pace and lead teams who feel overwhelmed, anxious and disconnected?

Operating from a place of influence and responsibility is a privilege. But let's be honest, it's also exhausting. Even for the most seasoned leaders, the pressure never really stops. Deadlines loom, expectations pile up and time feels more like a shrinking commodity than a supportive partner. Something has to give. And too often, that something is *you*.

It's a familiar story. One I've seen again and again. Leaders, business owners, executives who throw themselves into work, saying things like, *I'll start looking after myself next month*, or *I'll make it up to my family with a holiday*. But months pass, and nothing changes. The habit of work, accumulated over the years and often through watching parents or bosses, is deeply wired. It becomes who you are. And because it's rewarded, it becomes harder and harder to question.

You love the rush. The impact. The feeling of being needed. You're building something meaningful, and that matters. But beneath it all, something feels off. You just haven't had the time to stop and figure out what.

Let's Talk About Success...

Success is an interesting word; one that gets thrown around endlessly in leadership circles. For years, I thought success meant influence, money, status and strength. And in many ways, it did. I wore those markers like a badge of honour. I was proud of how much I could handle, how far I could push, how many problems I could solve. It felt like winning.

But over time, something started to shift. I realised that many of the people I admired—the ones with the titles, the recognition, the financial freedom—weren't always fulfilled. They were respected, yes. But many were exhausted, disconnected and quietly asking themselves, *Is this really it?*

That made me pause.

What does success really mean to you? Not the polished version. Not the version your LinkedIn profile projects. But the version that sits in your chest when the lights go off and no one's watching. What does it mean in the context of *life*?

Is it presence with your children? Is it inner peace when you wake up in the morning? Is it a relationship where you feel seen? A body that feels strong and calm? A sense of meaning in how you spend your hours?

Because here's the truth: success isn't always loud. It's not always public. Sometimes, it's soft, quiet and sacred.

If we're not careful, we can build our entire lives chasing someone else's version of success, only to find it doesn't satisfy the deeper ache.

So before we go any further, I want to ask you to hold this question close:

What does success really mean to you, now, in this season of your life?

Not what it meant five years ago. Not what it "should" mean. But what feels true today.

If you're not sure, that's okay. You're not behind. You're exactly where you need to be. Because asking this question, honestly and bravely, is the beginning of clarity. And clarity is the gateway to alignment.

And alignment is where real success begins.

Isn't it crazy how life just catches up on us? We spend our youth immersed in fun and freedom, but as we reach the edge of adulthood, everything changes. Suddenly, there's pressure to be someone, to make something of ourselves. We cross an invisible line into the world of expectation and achievement.

Before we know it, we're respected professionals, collecting the markers of success. We've got the titles, the responsibilities, the "things" to show for it. And for a while, we're proud to wear the mask of success. Why wouldn't we be? We're admired and praised; we feel like we've followed the path set out for us, and we've done it well.

But there's a crucial step missing along that path. Just like you'd check in at different stages of a major project to assess progress and pivot when needed, you must also check in with yourself. Without those check-ins, you risk building momentum on shaky foundations. You could be chasing the wrong goals, ignoring health issues, letting relationships drift or losing connection to what brings you joy.

Over time, if we don't stop to reflect and realign, we get lost. We lose the connection to who we are at our core. And when the wave of life builds too much momentum without us checking the direction, it's easy to drown in success that isn't even truly ours.

To be a great leader, it's essential to stay connected to your inner core. It deserves as much attention, care and strategy as your business does.

Foggy Mind, Foggy Life

It's not entirely our fault. The world we're born into is designed to distract and derail us. Culture, systems, social media and economic structures often serve larger powers; ones we don't understand but still shape our daily lives.

When your life is guided by external forces, you start making decisions that don't serve your best interests. The media tells you what to buy, how to think, what's trending and what to strive for. Bit by bit, you forget who you are.

The book *The Puppet Master's Bible* (Walker, 2024) explores how modern life manipulates us into becoming puppets in someone else's show. We're surrounded by messaging that looks like choice, but it's not. We're being curated. And that's why, even in success, we can feel empty.

Performing, achieving, firefighting, striving; it all adds up. And eventually, your brain goes into overload. Not because you're not capable, but because you're cognitively depleted.

Cognitive depletion happens when mental demand exceeds your brain's recovery. Like a smartphone battery running too many apps, you lose power. For leaders, it creeps in slowly…so slowly you don't notice until something breaks.

You forget appointments. You lose your keys. You drive off with your laptop on the roof of your car. You lose presence. And the cost? The cost is your life. The little moments you miss. The dog running in the park. Your kids playing in the next room. A laugh from your partner you don't hear because your mind is somewhere else.

Cognitive depletion narrows your view until all you can see is what's urgent. It robs you of the wide-angle lens that lets you lead with perspective.

To be a strong, conscious leader in today's world, you need to become your own puppet master; the master of your attention, your choices and your mental space.

Yes, AI will automate some tasks, but it will also demand higher-level thinking. Your brain must have the space and fuel to think deeply. Conscious attention is expensive. It drains energy fast. You must become selective, ruthless even. Block out anything not aligned with your purpose. And it starts with clarity.

The Power of Clarity

Clarity is often spoken about like a strategy tool, something you write down on a whiteboard or craft in a leadership retreat.

But real clarity comes from something deeper. It's that unshakeable inner knowing. The voice inside that says, *This is who I am. This is what matters. This is the direction I choose.*

When you lose that voice, you start making decisions from fear, pressure or comparison.

You chase what's urgent instead of what's important. You say yes to things that drain you. You pour your energy into solving the wrong problems.

If You Had One Month to Live...

Let's pause for a moment, not to analyse, but to feel.

If you found out today that you had just one month left to live, how would you spend it?

Would you keep up the same pace? Push through the same meetings, the same deadlines? Or would something quieter begin to rise; something more personal, more urgent?

Would you dance in the kitchen with your kids? Watch the sun melt into the ocean with someone you love? Write the letter you've been putting off? Laugh more? Say *no* more? Be present more?

This isn't a productivity exercise. It's a truth exercise. Because when everything unnecessary gets stripped away, what's left is what matters most.

This reflection isn't about fear, it's about clarity. Sometimes, we need to zoom all the way out to remember what's real. To realign. Not just with goals, but with what gives life meaning.

 Reflection Exercise

Set a timer for five minutes. In one stream-of-consciousness list, write down how you would spend your final month of life. Don't edit. Don't justify. Just write. Then circle three things you could honour in your life *this month,* without needing a crisis to act.

When I first did this exercise, I found it surprisingly difficult. After jotting down the standard answers, I hit a wall. It struck me how much of my life had been spent doing what I thought was expected. I had to keep asking, *And what else?* until I reached the parts of me I hadn't accessed in years.

Even if you only uncovered a sliver of your truth, that's a start. That moment of awareness is more powerful than you realise. Because for many people, especially leaders, we've buried parts of ourselves beneath performance and responsibility. Not because we're weak, but because we're human.

And humans protect what hurts. We put parts of our lives in boxes, lock them and throw away the key. But true leaders have the courage to go back, unlock the box and do the inner work. Not just to feel better, but to lead better.

Think about it: if this were your business, you'd make time to reflect, reset and realign. You'd build a solid strategy, review what worked and what didn't, and design a stronger foundation for the future. So why is it so hard to do that with your own life?

BALANCED SUCCESS

Hopefully that one-month reflection helped you begin to redefine it. Because the truth is, many people chase success by society's definition, only to reach it and feel unfulfilled. It's a hollow victory if it comes at the cost of your health, your relationships or your sense of self.

Success that isn't aligned with your values will eventually cost more than it gives.

This chapter is your wake-up call. Not to tear it all down, but to realign. To reconnect with the parts of you that got left behind along the way. And to begin rebuilding a definition of success that feels whole, honest and truly yours.

It isn't about judgement, it's about awareness. The pace of modern leadership can pull even the most grounded person off course. But the moment you stop to ask what success really means, and whether your current path reflects that, you've already begun the realignment.

You don't need to change everything overnight. You just need to pause long enough to ask the right questions. Because the most important work you'll ever do won't be measured in numbers or accolades. It will be how aligned your outer success is with your inner truth.

 Chapter Summary: A Wake-up Call to Realign

 Key Messages:

- Many leaders are high-performing, but disconnected.
- Traditional success is often loud but hollow.
- Clarity is the first step to reclaiming alignment.
- Misalignment compounds quietly until something breaks.

Actions to Take:

- Complete the "One Month to Live" reflection.
- Define what success means now, in this season.
- Honour one small part of your truth this week.
- Recognise that your real work isn't "out there". It's in here, in our hearts, minds and soul. And you're already on your way.

BALANCED SUCCESS

CHAPTER TWO

Born to Win, Wired to Perform

We are all the summary of our life experiences, and my own were the catalyst for writing this book.

I was eight years old, a little girl living in country New South Wales after moving from Western Australia. My Dad had just taken a shore-based navy role managing a Forces Career Office, and for the first time in a long time, we were all together. It felt like an adventure.

We lived near brooks and mountains, with snowy mountains visible from our backyard. One day I came home from school and announced I'd won the cross-country race. I'd never raced before. My Dad, a former champion runner, boxer, swimmer and cyclist, was thrilled. It must have been in my genes.

That day, Dad became my coach and a structured training plan appeared, military style.

Soon, I was winning regional and state championships. Weekends were full with Little Athletics or fun runs. I loved the rush, the thrill of winning, the time with Dad and the pride in his eyes.

Identity Formed Early

We used to run up the rocky mountain behind our house. It was brutal. I'd cry, and Dad would yell, *If you're going to cry, go home to your mother*. I'd keep going. He'd extend his hand, not as a rescue, but as a challenge: *Are you ready to keep going?* I always was.

Little did I know at the time that this rigorous training and competing was developing a deep foundation of resilience—a mindset to persevere and give my all—that would shape my adult years. Eventually, I started to fly. I won state titles in Victoria and NSW. When we returned to Perth, I found my true events: the 800m and 1500m. Speed and endurance, both tough and tactical. I trained hard, often in secret. I wanted to be the best.

When I was 12, I won the City to Surf 12 kilometre event in the under-13s category. Dad and I were invited to the Channel 7 studio for the awards ceremony, and we were both beaming. The local paper ran a story, and suddenly people started asking if I wanted to make the Sydney 2000 Olympics. I hadn't even thought about it, *I was still a kid, barely a teenager*. At 13, I peaked. Winning became who I was.

From the outside, everything looked great; loving family, beachside living, a simple life. But while other kids were playing, I was training, competing, living for the next event.

When I was selected to compete in Malaysia, I was overjoyed. But it was expensive. My parents offered a challenge: we'll make it happen if you help raise the funds. We ran a garage sale together. I have never forgotten the sacrifice and support of my family. That day symbolised what mattered: teamwork, belief and effort.

Then, at 16, everything changed. Hormones, boys, school stress. My body altered and my priorities shifted. A comment that I looked "pudgy" stuck. I spiralled. My identity as the lean, admired athlete collapsed. *Who was I, without the veneer of my version of "winning and success"?*

Behind the Curtain

Bulimia became my secret weapon; a way to eat and still stay small. My best friend at school was sporty like me, and I remember the day we came up with the plan together.

We would talk about it like it was any other topic we were interested in, but it wasn't. It became normal. We would challenge each other to see how long we could go without eating.

I was standing in the toilets at school in Year 11 in my bathers, before swimming class. I was lean, but I thought I was fat. I just kept looking in the mirror and felt sick at the idea I had to reveal my body to my classmates.

Bulimia gave me a twisted sense of control. It became my reliable companion, one that stayed by my side for over a decade. As I moved into my young adult years, outwardly I was thriving: a Sports Science degree and personal training qualifications. I was fit, healthy, capable. But the gym environment amplified my insecurities. I felt constant pressure to look a certain way, as if I were always on display. In a mostly young male setting, that pressure only deepened my struggle.

Inwardly, I felt lost. I needed to get away. To change something.

So I travelled the world for two years with my boyfriend. We backpacked our way around many countries, and gradually my zest for life returned. I found myself again. The disorder faded and I remembered that I was a winner.

When I returned to Perth, I landed what I thought was my dream job, working on youth sport and community programs for state government. I was just 24. My soon-to-be manager told me, *We've never hired someone so young for this role. Prove me right.*

Challenge accepted.

Government was slow, structured and hierarchical. I only knew one speed and it was fast. I had to switch lanes and conform. Eventually, I lost the fire.

At 28, I became an assistant manager in a large not-for-profit organisation. I had a team of 180 staff, and seven team leaders, all older than me. The reception? Cold. I was young, blonde, confident. They didn't welcome change, and they certainly didn't welcome me.

They called me the "white witch." Eventually, I went on stress leave. I left the job and I felt like a failure.

But I wasn't one to quit, and my grit kicked in. That little girl running up the mountain whispered in my ear, *You are a winner Tanya, find a way to create a successful career, no matter what.*

From Breakdown to Boldness

My partner, who became my husband, started an IT company. It was sudden. He was brilliant at technology, but not business. Luckily for me, I discovered I loved small business. The pace, the growth, the autonomy, leadership, the learning. I came alive again. I regained some of the sensations that had made me feel like a winner.

Our business grew fast. I hired a coach, read every book and watched every video. I treated business like I was training for a national championship. I was intense, focused and moved with pace. But things were shifting. The business started taking over everything, and I soon began to forget who I was and the things that mattered to me. I wore a mask to survive.

We had a big team, major clients, a flashy office. But it consumed us. Conversations became about work and my identity was now wrapped in the business. The mask I wore in the office started to stay on when I got home.

And slowly, I disappeared behind it.

I didn't realise how disconnected I'd become from myself, my values and my health. I was exhausted, anxious and questioning everything. I withdrew from friends and family and, with that, sealed my own fate: *You're going all in now. There is no turning back. It's business success all the way.*

Then one day over lunch we decided to move to New York and expand our IT company. It was far-fetched, ridiculous and spontaneous. In hindsight, it was escapism, on both sides. He casually presented the idea to me thinking I would laugh in his face. But I didn't. Perth felt small but I felt lost in it. A new adventure beckoned, in a city about as far as you can get from Perth.

When you're out of alignment, anything feels better than stillness.

New York City: Bold Moves and Breaking Points

It was a hard slog to get the business ready to operate without us physically there, in Perth. Starting a company on the other side of the world added another layer of stress. Friends and family thought we were mad. Most didn't think we'd actually go through with it.

But we did.

In June 2015, we boarded a plane, sat in our business class seats, and guzzled champagne like we'd just climbed Mount Everest. Little did I know, I had only arrived at base camp, and I didn't even have a map to get up the mountain.

When we arrived in New York, all we had was an Airbnb for a week, a few local contacts, and a recently opened U.S. bank account. We had no team, no network and no infrastructure, just the belief that we could build something from nothing. We had done it in Australia already; how hard could it be in NYC?

We set up in a WeWork space in Manhattan's Financial District. The pace of the city lit up something in me. There was no room for hesitation. We got scrappy and bold, bought a list of local business contacts, hired a digital agency to run a fast campaign, and hit the pavement hard. We'd pitch to anyone who'd listen.

One year in, our hard work paid off.

We won a major client, in fact, our biggest ever. Five offices across the USA, more than 180 staff, and a stunning head office in TriBeCa. It was everything we had dreamed of.

Our clients loved that we had a team in Australia for 24/7 support. We said *yes* on the spot, to everything and everyone, even before we'd figured out how we'd service them.

We scrambled. Found a white-label partner in Florida with the skills and staff to support the rollout. We made it happen, fast. It was a whirlwind of growth, pressure and hustle.

But amid the hustle, the familiar cracks began to show again. I was achieving, yes, but something was still missing. I was so full of adrenaline and busy-ness in the first year, I had forgotten that there was a deep and dark void in my soul. The business didn't feel like mine anymore.

Then it hit me: I was building someone else's dream; I was on a plane to their destination. And the worst part? Even if I got off, I didn't know my own journey. But I was in too deep at this point, so I kept going. A few years later, I became pregnant. I was 36, deeply unhappy, working around the clock, with no relief in sight. I'd never wanted to be a Mum; I thought I had more important things to do. But when I was pregnant, a light came on inside me. I had a new purpose, and it became my guiding light.

Then came a breach of trust; personal, painful and unexpected. It shattered something in me. The ground beneath me shifted yet again. I no longer felt safe in the life I was living.

The mask cracked. And everything I'd been avoiding rose to the surface.

In the months that followed, my health collapsed. I was heavily pregnant, alone most days, and barely functioning. My body shut down from exhaustion. I found myself lying on the couch in the dark for weeks at a time, still running the business from my phone. I was surviving, but only just.

A simple act, drinking a glass of hot water with salt, brought me back to life in a small way. I'd been severely sodium deficient. The symbolism wasn't lost on me. I was depleted in every way.

Then the lowest point in my life happened. I was seven months pregnant and decided to move out of our apartment in the Financial District in Manhattan. The stress had become too much. The only thing was, I had nowhere to go. So, I stayed in Airbnbs for a night or two at a time. It was a costly undertaking in NYC, but I felt like I had no other choice.

I would walk through the streets in the midst of summer, humid and boiling, with my big bag of clothes. I would move from one place to another, all whilst running our business.

My phone never stopped.

I was astonished to realise that I was a displaced pregnant women, alone, with no plan to hand over my business responsibilities. *How had it come to this?*

Eventually, I left the relationship. Quietly, without drama. I chose my peace. I chose my daughter. And I began the slow, painful process of realignment.

However, the hits kept coming, although they weren't as direct. COVID hit. The borders were closing. I didn't think twice. I booked a one-way flight to Perth. One suitcase. One baby. No plan. I sobbed for eight hours at John F Kennedy airport, leaving our dog behind with the babysitter. I just knew I had to go.

Thirty-six hours later, I landed in Perth. My parents' home felt like a sanctuary. It was the first time in years I had space to breathe. No business chaos. No broken relationship. Just me, my daughter and a blank slate.

It wasn't dramatic; it was subtle. A slow unravelling that brought me back to truth, to health, to what really matters.

Perspective Returns

For the first time in years, I wasn't in survival mode. And with that space came the most powerful gift: perspective.

I asked myself: *Why did it take me this long to get here?*

I thought I was smart. Self-aware. But when your mind is constantly on—work, social media, noise—there's no space for reflection. And without space, there is no clarity.

Without clarity, there's no alignment.

And without alignment, even the most successful life can feel empty.

 Chapter Summary: Born to Win, Wired to Perform

 Key Messages:

- High performance can build identity, but also mask disconnection.
- Unprocessed pain creates hidden behaviours that sabotage wellbeing.
- Sometimes, reinvention comes not from success, but from collapse.
- Realignment requires honesty, stillness and courage to choose peace.

 Actions to Take:

- Reflect on moments when performance defined your identity.
- Where in your life have you worn a mask?
- What's one story you're ready to release, so a truer one can begin?
- Remember: Your origin story shaped you. But it doesn't have to define your future. You get to choose who you become next.

CHAPTER THREE

Creating the Destination and

Upgrading the Plane

The Wake-Up Call

Author and disability rights advocate Helen Keller once remarked: *"The only thing worse than being blind is having sight but no vision"*.

The first step is asking: *Where am I actually headed?*

Most leaders have a clear business vision. It's likely the result of countless hours of research, strategic conversations and careful planning. This provides purpose and direction, crucial for strategic clarity and success.

> But what about a personal vision? This isn't something most people think about. And yet, it holds more weight than a business plan ever could.

Somewhere along the line, we stopped zooming out to see our life as a complete picture. We became short-sighted, focused on phases: young adulthood, mid-career, retirement. But life isn't lived in phases. It's lived in moments. And when we don't create a vision for our whole life, we miss important pieces.

That's a huge blind spot. Because if your plane is flying full-speed without a destination, you're gambling with your future.

I created a simple yet powerful exercise that is helping my clients shift their mindset:

A Letter From Your 80-Year-Old Self

Imagine you're 80. You've lived a full life. What would that wise version of you say to you now?

Prompts to guide you:

- What mattered most in the end?
- What brought you joy, peace, pride?
- What do you wish you had done more, or less, of?
- What would you tell the "you" of today?

From my own letter:

Those girls of yours they won't always be small. That idea in your heart, you won't always have the energy to pursue it. Time is your most precious currency. Spend it where it counts.

Lead with love. Speak the truth, even when your voice shakes. Be bold in your becoming. The life you want is on the other side of alignment, not achievement.

Take the time, and don't overthink it. Let this reconnect you with your inner compass.

Strip back the noise. Remember who you were before the world told you who to be.

The Unspoken Cost

For years, I wore success like a badge. My days were filled with strategy sessions and late nights. I thought I was doing it right. I thought leaders sacrificed, and I was proud of my ability to push through.

But when I was in labour, lying in a hospital bed, still replying to emails with no one by my side, that's when it hit me. It wasn't even a feeling that I had been abandoned; rather, that I had completely abandoned myself.

It had been building for years. I missed family events, friend catch-ups and time with people I loved, all in the name of business. And I was praised for it, however the praise stopped meaning anything.

Eventually, something cracked. Not a big public breakdown, but a quiet voice inside saying: *This isn't it.*

That was my real wake-up call.

The Power of Perspective

Take a look again at how you'd spend your last month alive. What's a simple word that can define it? Grateful? Sad? Regretful? Proud?

Whatever comes up, that's your soul speaking.

Misalignment isn't always loud. It might be tension with your partner, unexplained headaches, creeping weight gain or risky decisions. They seem small, but they're signals.

You're flying a plane full-speed without checking your fuel, your altitude or your destination. Eventually, something breaks.

BALANCED SUCCESS

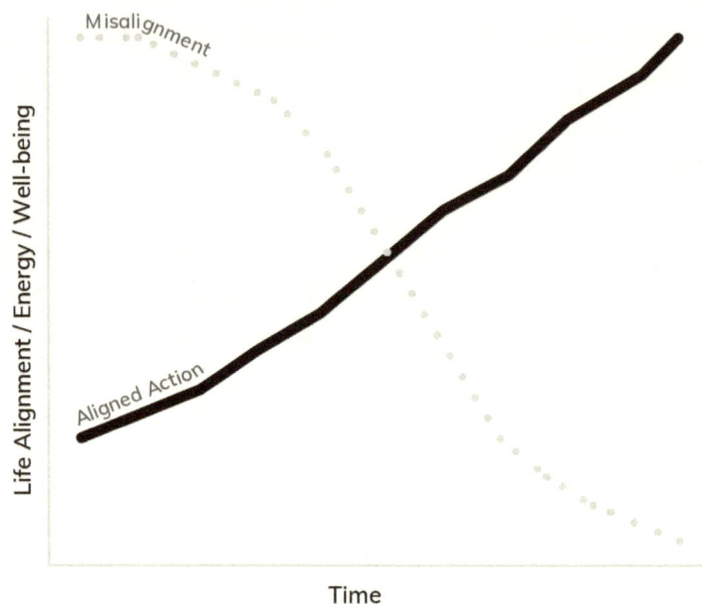

This graph shows what I call the compounding cost of misalignment. In the beginning, you might feel fine. But small misalignments add up, until the line drops steeply. That's where burnout, illness or disconnection hits.

But there's also another line, the upward curve. That's what happens when you start taking small, aligned actions. Tiny steps. Daily wins. Over time, those choices compound too. That's the path to *Balanced Success*.

**You don't drift into alignment,
you design it.**

Reverse-Engineering Your Vision

Ask yourself:
- After your career ends, what five things will matter most? *For example: joy, health, or family.*
- List three to five actions that will support those outcomes. *For example: for joy, it might be a monthly games night with the family.*
- Rank each: On Track / Kind of / Off Track

This alone can shift everything.

We plan meetings, launches, even funerals, but rarely do we design a life that feels deeply aligned at the end.

The most fulfilled leaders I know aren't the richest. They're the clearest.

Where Is Your Plane Headed?

If your life was a plane, what's the destination?

Are you flying on autopilot? Or have you set a course that feels aligned?

Because no matter how fast you're going, if you're heading in the wrong direction, speed doesn't help.

The 10x10 Life Grid

Map your life in squares to gain perspective on where you've been and what's left.

How to Use It

- The grid has **100 squares**: **1 square = 1 year**.
- Read it **left to right, top to bottom** (like a book).
    > Top row = ages **0–9**, next row **10–19** … bottom row **90–99**.

Steps

- **Choose a target lifespan.**
  You can use Australian averages of **85.3 years for women, 81.2 years for men** (ABS, 2023), or pick your own based on family history and goals.
- **Mark your target age.**
  Find the square that matches your target final year and **outline or star it**. This is your "finish line."
- **Shade what's already lived.**
  Count from age 0 up to your **current age** and **shade those squares**. This shows the years you've already lived.
- **Optional: show likely remaining years.**
  From the square **after your current age** up to your target age, **cross-hatch** or use a different pattern.
  Leave any squares **beyond** your target age unshaded (think of these as **bonus years**).

Legend (suggested)

- ● Shaded = years lived
- ▧ Cross-hatched = likely remaining (to target age)
- ○ Blank = bonus years (beyond target)

Note: Averages are not predictions. Use this as a perspective tool, without pressure, to focus your time on what matters most.

This exercise is about more than just simple maths. It's about perspective.

It's a powerful, and sometimes confronting, reminder that our time on this planet is limited. If there's something you truly want, go after it now. Don't wait for the perfect moment. That moment is *now*.

You are the author of your life. Make sure you're writing a story that feels true, bold and yours.

10 x 10 Life Grid
Each Square = 1 Year

You are the author of your life. Make sure you're writing a story that feels true, bold and yours.

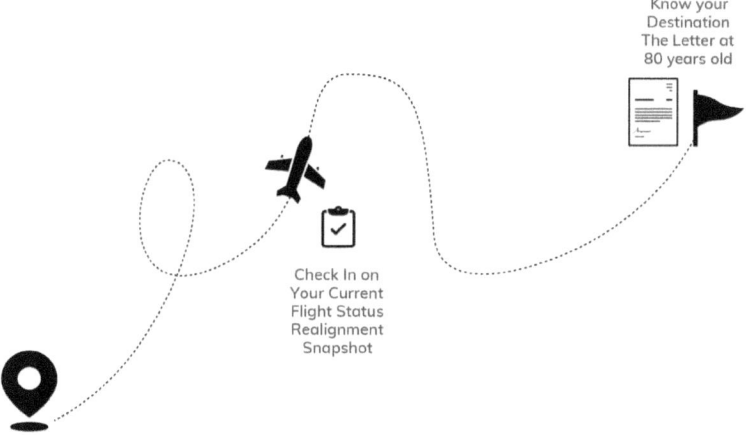

Chapter Summary: Creating the Destination and Upgrading the Plane

 Key Messages:

- Business vision without personal vision creates misalignment.
- Future-you holds the wisdom you need today.
- Misalignment compounds, but so does intentional alignment.
- You are always one decision away from redesigning your life.

 Actions to Take:

- Write a letter from your 80-year-old self.
- List your top five end-of-life priorities.
- Identify which areas are off track and why.
- Remember: The plane is in motion, and you are the pilot.

CHAPTER FOUR

Redefining Success

I worked all day from my office in Manhattan five days a week, and then from my apartment after hours and on weekends. The hours were long, and it was rarely enjoyable or rewarding. I coordinated engineers to resolve client issues hour after hour, managed everything on the business end, and oversaw strategic operations back in Australia. But the hardest part wasn't the work, it was watching my business partner and then-husband lose himself.

Slowly, I watched him slip further away, emotionally and mentally, until he was barely recognisable.

I can handle deadlines. I can handle chaos. I even thrive in the face of a business challenge. But what I experienced in Manhattan revealed something deeper. At first, I threw myself into the energy of the city.

BALANCED SUCCESS

Everyone seemed so smart, so driven. There were no boundaries between work and life, just one fast-paced, never-ending cycle of business and success. It was intense. And for a while, it was also exhilarating.

But something monumental was missing: **Balance.**

How can you create a sustainable and happy life built only on business and adrenaline? You can't. Eventually, the other essential parts of life catch up with you. And if you ignore them long enough, they come crashing down.

The Evolution of Success

What does success mean to you now? Think about the current chapter of your life, not your past, not your LinkedIn bio, not the version others applaud. Right now, in this season, what does a successful life actually feel like to you? Does it energize or exhaust you? Does it align with your values, or just your calendar?

Many leaders operate in what I call The Old Success Paradigm, a model built on relentless achievement, constant output, external validation and dopamine-chasing busyness. On the surface, they appear confident and accomplished. But deep inside, something vital is misaligned. Their drive may win them awards, titles and recognition, but their soul is quietly suffocating.

What we're shifting towards in this book is a model I call ***Balanced Success***.

Think of the classic iceberg metaphor. On the left, there is the traditional view of success: above the waterline are things like money, material possessions, titles and accomplishments. But beneath the surface lies a foundation built on stress, long hours and the habit of prioritising work over everything else.

On the right is a different version, a more aligned one. Here, success still includes business growth and achievement, but it's fuelled by a deeper connection to self, vitality and joy. Beneath the surface is what truly sustains long-term fulfilment: rest, boundaries, purpose, self-awareness and wellbeing.

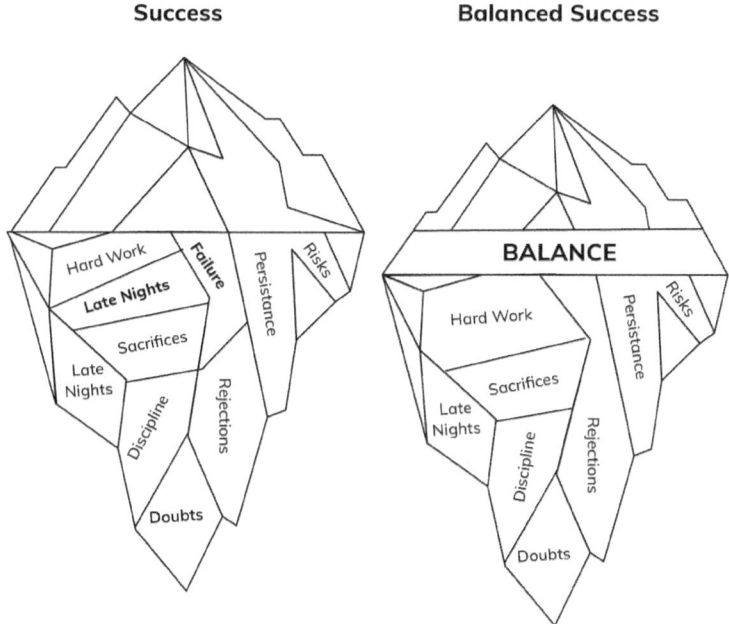

Balanced Success is about knowing where you're headed and consciously balancing the essential components of your life that help you get there. It's the understanding that true success doesn't come from one area alone; it's the result of focus and energy invested across *all* areas of life. And when those areas work in harmony, something powerful happens.

You become someone deeply connected to your soul. Your vitality becomes infectious. You move through life with strength, presence, clarity and purpose.

Living a balanced life doesn't happen by chance. Like anything meaningful, it takes time, intention and consistency. Most of us have a few areas we tend to neglect or avoid. Part of the *Balanced Success* journey is uncovering why. And almost always, the challenges relate to the relationship we have with ourselves.

The real work is digging up what's been buried, understanding the reason it was pushed aside and then committing to bring it back into the light, consistently, so it can support the life you truly want to live.

The real work is deliberate, sustained change, not a quick fix. For me it wasn't a quick process. My journey of self-discovery, reuniting with myself, and rebuilding from the inside out spanned several years. I didn't do it alone, and I wouldn't have come this far if I'd tried to.

I found people who were aligned with what I needed; coaches, mentors and friends. It was an ongoing commitment: time, energy, money and, above all, a willingness to let go and peel back the layers. I made many sacrifices, and let me tell you, it was difficult, uncomfortable and raw.

But as many of you know, this is when the real growth happens.

When I arrived at the stage where my identity was changing, my values were shifting, and I started to look at the world around me in a whole different way, I was both scared and excited. I was transforming into a new version of myself.

I still continue this work now, less as emergency triage and more as maintenance and expansion, because I believe we all need to tend to our inner world just as we do our physical health. For me, that looks like daily practices, honest check-ins, supportive relationships, and course corrections when I drift. Growth isn't a destination; it's a rhythm. Tending the inner world keeps me steady and kind, and it lets me lead with clarity, on the days that feel light, and especially on the days that don't.

What that 'real work' looked like for me:

- Coaching for accountability and blind spots.
- Values work and rewriting unhelpful beliefs.
- Nervous-system care: sleep, nutrition, movement, breathwork.
- Boundaries, saying *no*, and simplifying commitments.
- Reflection practices: journaling, check-ins, meditation/visualisation.

- Repairing key relationships and building supportive ones.

Here's a snapshot of how the old and new paradigms might compare:

Old Version of Success	Balanced Success
Hustle and grind culture	Sustainable energy and focused intention
Productivity and output are everything	Presence, impact, and alignment are key
Success = status, money, recognition	Success = values, meaning, legacy
Sacrifice is seen as strength	Self-respect and boundaries are honoured
Constant availability	Time freedom and self-leadership
Performance at the cost of well-being	Well-being as a core part of performance
External validation drives decisions	Inner compass drives decisions
More is better	Enough is powerful

For years, I lived by the old version of success: strive, achieve, repeat. I ticked the boxes, I pushed through exhaustion, I built businesses and hit milestones, but somewhere along the way, I lost touch with myself. Maybe you have too.

What *Balanced Success* **Actually Means**

Balanced Success isn't about doing less, it's about doing the *right* things, with clarity, intention and alignment. It's recognising that your energy is your greatest currency. It's about building something meaningful without abandoning yourself in the process.

It means being successful *and* fulfilled. Driving results *and* staying well. Leading a business *and* living a life.

I created the *Balanced Success Wheel* to help you redefine what a truly successful life looks and feels like, on your terms. It's not a one-size-fits-all balance model. It's a living framework born from personal

BALANCED SUCCESS

transformation and real work with leaders.

Each part of this wheel represents a vital area of life. When aligned, you lead from wholeness, not hustle. The wheel gives you a clear picture of where you're strong, where you're stretched, and where you may be sacrificing your wellbeing for goals that no longer serve you.

Success doesn't have to feel like survival.

In the pages ahead, you'll explore the eight core areas of *Balanced*

Success. You'll be invited to reflect, recalibrate and realign your life. Not so it looks good from the outside, but so it feels right on the inside.

Because when you feel strong in your body, clear in your mind, supported in your relationships, aligned in your work and connected to something greater, that's not just success. That's *Balanced Success*.

1. **Health & Vitality.** The foundation that fuels everything. Your physical health is your first wealth. Without it, all other areas suffer. This area includes movement, sleep, nourishment, hydration, breathwork, nervous system regulation and rest. This is about building a body that supports your energy and longevity, so you can show up for the life you're here to lead.
2. **Mental Wealth.** Your inner operating system. This is the state of your mind, resilience, clarity, emotional regulation and identity. It's shaped through self-awareness, mental hygiene, intentional habits and mindset. When this area is strong, you respond instead of react and lead from calm, not chaos.
3. **Growth & Contribution.** Becoming more so you can give more. Growth is your ongoing evolution. Contribution is how you use your growth to lift others. *Balanced Success* invites both: becoming your best and sharing your best with the world.
4. **Connection.** Success means nothing without connection. Your relationships reflect how deeply you're connected to yourself. This area includes your partner, family, friendships and community. Connection is where love, support and emotional safety reside. Humans are wired for belonging.
5. **Abundance & Finance:** The engine of choice and stability. Abundance is the mindset, finance is the method. This area is about clarity, conscious decisions and simple money systems. When your money aligns with your values, you create freedom, reduce stress and build long-term confidence.
6. **Fun, Joy & Creativity.** Fuel for your soul and nervous system. Fun isn't a luxury, it's vital. This area is about play, lightness and

creativity. Joy regulates your nervous system, boosts innovation and keeps life vibrant.
7. **Business & Career.** Your platform for purpose and contribution. This is your work in the world. It's about aligning your strengths and purpose with a professional path that inspires you. Fulfilment comes from growth, contribution and impact, not just recognition.
8. **Spiritual Alignment.** Your deeper connection and internal compass. This is your connection to something bigger, whether that's nature, God, the universe or your higher self. Spiritual alignment is where you find peace, guidance and perspective beyond logic.

Balanced success isn't an abstract ideal; it's a lived experience, and now you have the map in your hands. This model is here to guide you, challenge you and remind you of what truly matters when life gets busy or noisy.

From here, we'll go deeper into each part of the model, exploring what alignment looks like—and what misalignment feels like—in real life.

This isn't about fixing you. It's about reconnecting you to the version of yourself that's already whole, already wise and already capable of creating a life that feels as good as it looks.

 Chapter Summary: Redefining Success

 Key Messages:

- True success isn't just about achievement, it's about alignment.
- The old model of hustle and status often leads to burnout and emptiness.
- *Balanced Success* invites you to lead with intention, values and energy that lasts.
- The *Balanced Success Wheel* introduces eight core life areas to assess and realign.

- Your energy, clarity and purpose are your most powerful leadership tools.

Your Next Step:

Rate yourself in each of the eight core areas using the *Balanced Success Baseline*. Start where you feel the most out of alignment and use this book as your guide back to wholeness.

Your Map Is Set, Now Let's Walk It.

You don't have to read the next chapters in order. If there's a particular area that feels like a gap or needs your attention right now, start there. This book was designed to meet you where you're at. But I encourage you to come back to the other areas too; even one insight might shift something big.

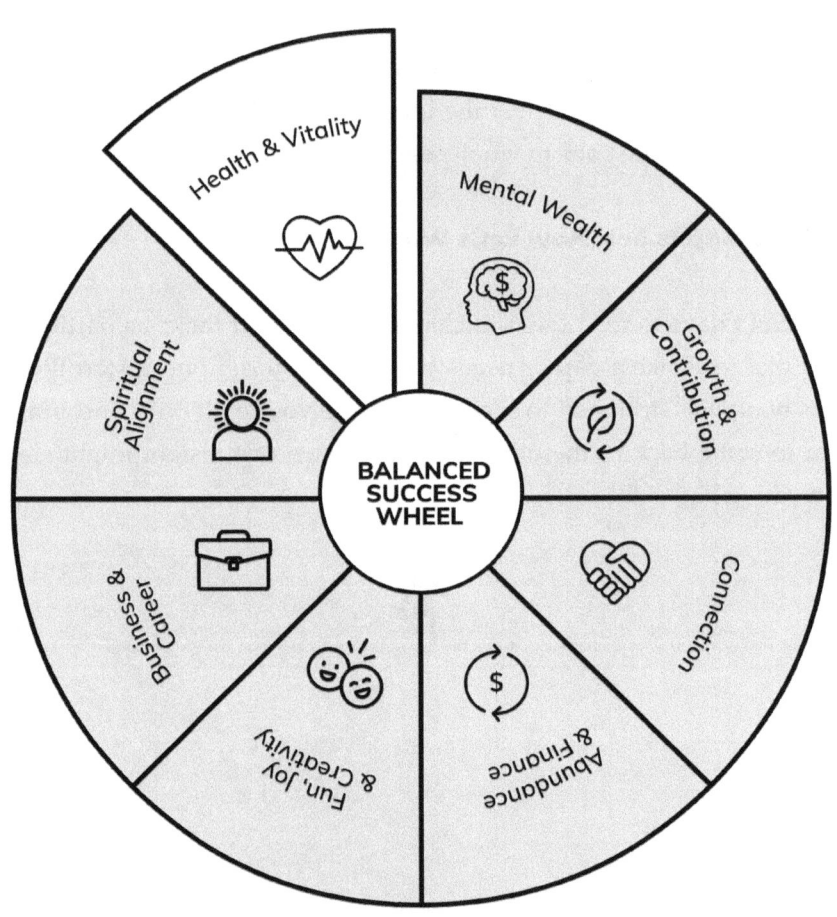

CHAPTER FIVE

Health & Vitality

If I had to choose one area of the *Balanced Success Wheel* as being the most important, it would be this one. Because if you don't have your health, everything else suffers. Your clarity, your energy, your ability to show up for others, your resilience under pressure…all of it.

Yet for so many leaders, health becomes an afterthought.

We chase success, push through stress, and tell ourselves we'll take care of ourselves "later". But later often arrives in the form of a wake-up call; burnout, illness, exhaustion or a life event that forces us to stop.

Let me be clear: not prioritising your health now is playing a deadly game of rolling the dice. You only get one body, one mind, one nervous system. If you burn through all your resources now, there might not be much left when you finally get around to yourself.

It's time to make health a non-negotiable.

Health is My Priority

Health has been woven into my life from the beginning. I grew up with wholesome, real food. Think veggie gardens, chickens and home-cooked meals. That foundation continued through my years as a state-level middle-distance runner, then as a Sports Science graduate and certified personal trainer. I've studied health, lived it, taught it…and at times, lost it.

Like many people, I've had seasons where health was compromised for achievement. But what I've come to realise is this:

Health isn't just one part of success, it's the foundation of it.

There are endless fads, diets, programs and influencers telling you what to do. But for leaders, particularly those balancing a business, a team, a family or a vision, what matters most is a whole-life approach.

In this chapter, we'll look at the four health pillars that are essential to long-term leadership:

1. **Nutrition**
2. **Exercise**
3. **Sleep and Recovery**
4. **Eliminating Toxins**

A Note About the Importance of Telomeres in Our Longevity

Before we dive into the four key pillars of health, I want to share something I believe every leader should understand—telomeres.

Telomeres are like protective caps at the ends of your chromosomes. Imagine the plastic tips at the end of your shoelaces that stop them from fraying. That's essentially what telomeres do for your DNA. They protect your genetic material every time your cells divide.

But here's the part that matters for you: as we age, our telomeres naturally shorten. The faster they shorten, the faster we age, not just in appearance, but in our biological health. Shortened telomeres have been linked to chronic conditions such as cancer, cardiovascular disease and cognitive decline.

The good news? Your lifestyle choices can influence the rate of telomere shortening.

According to Nobel Prize-winning researcher Dr. Elizabeth Blackburn and health psychologist Dr. Elissa Epel, the length of your telomeres, and thus your biological aging process, is not fixed. *The Telomere Effect* (Blackburn and Epel, 2017) explains that certain behaviours can slow, halt and in some cases, even reverse the shortening of telomeres. This includes:

- Eating a nutrient-rich, anti-inflammatory diet.
- Engaging in regular physical activity.
- Prioritising quality sleep and recovery.
- Managing psychological stress.
- Building meaningful relationships and cultivating purpose.

> *"Your cells are listening to your thoughts. Your telomeres are listening to your habits."*
> **- The Telomere Effect**

Why does this matter in a book about *Balanced Success*?

Because the work you do in your business, your leadership and your family requires more than just ambition. It requires sustainable vitality.

BALANCED SUCCESS

This isn't about aesthetics or temporary wellness trends. This is about longevity with energy and clarity, so you can keep showing up, leading effectively and enjoying your life for decades to come.

Understanding the science of telomeres reminds us that every choice we make, including what we eat, how we move, how we recover and how we think, has a ripple effect down to a cellular level. That's powerful.

So as we explore nutrition, exercise, sleep and recovery and eliminating toxins I invite you to not just see these as habits to tick off, but as long-term investments in your future self.

Now let's begin with food, because what you eat either fuels or fatigues you.

Nutrition: The Foundation of Balanced Success

A quick disclaimer: while I am a sports scientist and personal trainer, I am neither a doctor nor a dietician. However, my life and career experiences have given me excellent insights into what's important nutritionally, in ensuring alignment.

The adage, *you are what you eat*, holds profound truth. In today's fast-paced world, unless you're preparing meals yourself and understanding their origins, it's challenging to ascertain their healthfulness. Many processed foods are laden with hidden sugars, unhealthy fats and additives that can undermine well-being.

The food industry often markets products as "healthy" or "natural", yet many of these claims are misleading. Relying heavily on restaurant meals or pre-packaged foods places trust in establishments whose primary goals might not align with optimal nutrition.

While dining out occasionally is practical and enjoyable, it's essential to recognise that nutrition isn't a luxury; it's a necessity. Inconsistent eating patterns, such as alternating between restrictive diets and indulgent meals, can disrupt metabolic balance and overall health.

Life is meant to be savoured, including the occasional indulgence. However, consistency is key. Prioritizing whole, nutrient-dense foods should be the norm, with treats being the exception.

Key Areas of Focus
Gut Health: Your Inner Ecosystem

In recent years, the significance of gut health has become increasingly evident. Professor Tim Spector, a leading expert in genetic epidemiology and co-founder of the ZOE nutrition project, emphasizes that our gut microbiome—a diverse community of trillions of microorganisms—plays a pivotal role in our overall well-being. Disruptions in this microbial community have been linked to everything from chronic inflammation and fatigue to low mood, cognitive fog and even depression.

The Microbiome: Your Internal Pharmacy

Spector often describes the gut microbiome as an "internal ecosystem" or a "natural pharmacy" that produces chemicals which influence our immune system, hormone regulation and brain function. When well-fed, these microbes help regulate everything from stress to sleep to blood sugar. But when they're starved of real food, or overwhelmed by ultra-processed alternatives, the system begins to malfunction.

Diversity is Key

One of the most important markers of a healthy gut is diversity. Spector recommends aiming for 30+ different plant-based foods each week; not just fruits and vegetables, but herbs, spices, legumes, nuts and seeds. These feed a broad spectrum of good gut bacteria, helping to reduce inflammation, support digestion and enhance overall vitality.

Getting Started with Gut Health

If you've never taken a gut-focused approach to your diet before, don't worry; you don't need to overhaul your life overnight. The key is to start small, stay consistent and be kind to yourself in the process. Think of this as a long-term investment in your energy, clarity and vitality.

Here are a few simple starting points:

- **Add, don't restrict** – Instead of focusing on what to remove, begin by adding more variety of plants to your meals. Aim for the 30+ plants per week rule (including herbs, spices, nuts, seeds, fruit, veg, legumes and grains).
- **Read labels mindfully** – Start noticing what's in your food. If it has a long list of unrecognisable ingredients or added sugars, it may be worth reconsidering.

- **Go slow with fibre** – If your current diet is low in fibre, introduce new foods gradually. Too much too fast can cause bloating or discomfort.
- **Hydrate generously** – Water is essential to help fibre move through your system and support digestion.
- **Listen to your body** – Every gut is unique. Notice how you feel after meals. Do certain foods give you energy or leave you feeling sluggish?

Most importantly, if you've experienced chronic bloating, fatigue, skin issues, brain fog or autoimmune symptoms, it may be a sign your gut needs more focused care. In those cases, it's wise to speak to a qualified nutritionist, naturopath or integrative doctor who understands gut health. They can help you with testing, tailored plans, and strategies to restore your microbiome safely.

This isn't about perfection. It's about building a new normal that supports a thriving internal environment. Because when your gut is in good shape, the rest of your life often follows.

By treating your gut like the central command centre it truly is, you'll experience more energy, better clarity, and long-term physical resilience. And that, to me, is real success; it's not about control or restriction, it's about alignment with what helps you thrive.

Whole Foods – Seasonal and Locally Sourced

"Go to the farmers market and familiarize yourself with each season's produce."
- Samin Nosrat (chef, author)

One of the simplest ways to reconnect with your health is to reconnect with your food—where it comes from, how it's grown and who grows it. In today's world, convenience has become king. Supermarkets offer year-round access to just about everything, but it often comes at the cost of freshness, quality and nutrient density.

When you eat whole foods, those that are close to their natural state, you're choosing nourishment over processing. These foods tend to be richer in nutrients, free from additives and preservatives and more aligned with how the human body was designed to eat. Fresh fruit, vegetables, legumes, grains, meat and fish all fall into this category. And when sourced locally and in season, they not only taste better, but they carry fewer food miles, retain more nutrients and usually require less chemical intervention to grow and store.

Tanya's Tips for Eating Well

In our household, Sunday mornings are reserved for the local farmers market. It's become a ritual in our home, and my two girls are part of the process. They help make the shopping list, walk around the stalls with me, ask questions and learn about food. It's not just about groceries; it's about education, connection and building good habits early. My daughters are learning that real food doesn't come in boxes; it comes from soil, sun, water and care.

For our proteins, I use a subscription service that sources grass-fed beef and ocean-caught fish directly from farms and fisheries that practice sustainable and ethical farming. I know where our food is coming from and trust the quality.

And yes, I still shop at supermarkets when I need to, but I follow a simple rule: If it has a long list of ingredients, especially ones I can't pronounce, it's probably not good for me. My preference is always for whole foods. If I pick up something in a packet, I flip it over and check the back. If it's full of additives or sweeteners, I put it back. Your body knows the difference, even if your taste buds have been trained to ignore it.

Eating whole, seasonal and local doesn't mean you have to restock your pantry overnight. Small steps done consistently lead to the biggest results. Here are a few ways to begin:

- Start with one meal a day. Pick breakfast or dinner and aim to make it from whole ingredients such as vegetables, eggs, whole grains, fresh herbs and simple proteins.
- Shop the perimeter of the supermarket. That's where the real food lives—fruits, vegetables, meat, dairy and bakery. The inner aisles are mostly full of packaged and processed food.
- Read the back of the packet. If you can't pronounce an ingredient or you wouldn't find it in a home kitchen, think twice. Real food doesn't come with a long ingredient list.
- Visit your local farmers market. This is one of the easiest ways to eat what's in season and support your local community. Talk to the growers. Build relationships. Ask questions.
- Cook simply. You don't need fancy techniques or a pantry full of superfoods. Roasted vegetables with olive oil, a piece of grass-fed meat and some fresh herbs go a long way.
- Get the family involved. Whether it's writing the shopping list, picking produce, or helping stir the pot, involvement is how healthy habits get passed down through generations.
- Make food enjoyable, not stressful. Whole food isn't about restriction. It's about nourishment. Think like Jamie Oliver; make it joyful, colourful and bursting with flavour.

Gut health has become a non-negotiable part of my daily routine. Like many of you, I once underestimated its impact—until I started paying attention to how I felt. These are now some of my simple go-to gut-supporting practices:

- Add vegetables to every meal (well, almost every meal). One of my daily non-negotiables is making sure I get as many vegetables into my meals as possible. It's a simple habit that makes a huge difference to gut health, and it's easier than most people think.

- For breakfast, I often enjoy a slice of sourdough topped with avocado, fresh sliced tomato and a generous sprinkle of seeds. It's delicious, satisfying and packed with fibre and nutrients to kick-start the day.
- Even when ordering out, I make choices that support my gut. At my local Vietnamese spot, I always ask for a pho with vegetables instead of noodles; it's light, flavourful and leaves me feeling amazing. And when eating at cafes or restaurants, I'll often ask to swap chips for a fresh salad or extra greens. You'd be surprised how many places are happy to accommodate when you simply ask.
- Think about the small, consistent swaps that add up. When vegetables are the base of your plate, your gut and your energy level will thank you.

Gut-Smart Guidelines

If you want to nurture your microbiome:
- Eat a variety of plants each week (aim for 30+).
- Include fermented foods like kimchi, kefir or sauerkraut.
- Stay hydrated; your gut bugs need water too.
- Minimise ultra-processed and refined foods.
- Try time-restricted eating (10-12 hour food window). See below section about fasting for more information.

> *"Real food doesn't have ingredients, real food is ingredients."*
> **– Jamie Oliver**

Whole food eating isn't about perfection; it's about quality, consistency and building a strong foundation for your health. The more you know your food, the more you respect what you put into your body. And when you involve your family, you're creating ripple effects that can last generations.

Glucose: The Silent Driver of Energy, Mood and Long-Term Health

You are what you eat, but more specifically, you are how your body responds to what you eat. At the heart of that response is glucose, your body's main energy source. When glucose levels spike and crash, they don't just impact energy; they affect your mood, sleep, hormones, cravings, inflammation and long-term health.

I learned this the hard way.

In the past, I ate based on convenience and cravings. Then I went all-in on the keto diet, cutting out almost all carbs and focusing on high-fat foods. It helped me lose weight quickly, but it wasn't sustainable. I missed variety, especially vegetables, and I struggled to get the right balance. That experience taught me that extremes aren't the answer; consistency is.

Now, I follow a Mediterranean-style diet: lean protein, loads of vegetables, healthy fats like olive oil and a small amount of slow-burning carbs. I rarely eat dessert, not because I'm being "disciplined", but because my dinner is satisfying, delicious and leaves me genuinely full. I no longer ride the rollercoaster of energy highs and lows.

Instead, I focus on glucose-friendly living, and it has made a huge difference to how I feel day to day.

Why Glucose Management Matters

Glucose is a simple sugar that provides the body's key source of energy. Carbohydrates are broken down in our body into glucose, which then provides cell energy.

Managing your glucose isn't just about weight, it's about:
- **Mood stability** – Avoiding sugar crashes that lead to irritability or anxiety.
- **Energy and focus** – No more brain fog or 3pm slumps.
- **Hormonal balance** – Supporting insulin sensitivity, stress

hormones and even sleep quality.
- **Craving control** – Preventing the cycle of needing sugar to feel "normal".
- **Long-term health** – Protecting against chronic inflammation, Type 2 diabetes and other preventable conditions.

Tanya's Glucose Tips: Simple Changes that Changed my Life

A huge influence for me in this area was Jessie Inchauspé, the *Glucose Goddess*, whose tips brought science into simple habits anyone can adopt. I use many of her practices:
- I eat vegetables first, followed by protein and healthy fat, with carbs last.
- I avoid naked carbs and instead always pair them with a fat or protein to slow glucose release.
- I often go for a walk after dinner, especially with my kids, which is a great way to reduce glucose spikes while spending time together.
- I skip dessert most nights, not out of restriction, but because I feel nourished and stable.

If this is new territory for you, don't worry. Start small:
- **Observe how you feel** after meals. Notice any dips in energy, cravings or fogginess.
- **Swap out refined carbs** such as white bread and baked goods for more complex, fibre-rich ones like oats, legumes, or quinoa.
- **Add protein and fibre** to every meal. This slows glucose absorption and keeps you full for longer.
- **Cook at home more often**, even just a few times a week. It gives you full control over ingredients and quality.
- **Invest in tools such as a pressure cooker or slow cooker** to make real food easy and time-efficient.

And as always, speak to a health professional or dietitian if you have specific needs or want help tailoring your approach.

> Stabilising your glucose is the silent key to unlocking consistent energy, stable moods and long-term health, and it starts with the choices you make every day.

Fasting: A Forgotten Human Superpower

Let's rewind to the beginning.

Long before food delivery apps, 24/7 supermarkets, or morning smoothies, our ancestors lived in sync with nature. Food was something you *hunted* or *gathered*, not something that appeared in a box or from a drive-thru. That meant there were regular periods of feast *and* famine, and surprisingly, those fasting windows were not detrimental. They were actually biologically beneficial.

Fast forward to today: we eat from the moment we wake until the moment we go to bed.

Many people consume five or six meals or snacks a day without ever giving their bodies a break. Yet, our physiology hasn't evolved much from those prehistoric human days. Our bodies are still designed to handle periods without food, and in fact, thrive in them.

Fasting isn't a new health trend. It's a forgotten biological rhythm.

What the Research Says

Emerging studies in metabolic health and longevity show that intermittent fasting (or time-restricted eating) gives the body time to rest, repair and regenerate. According to Dr. Valter Longo, a leading researcher in fasting and longevity, fasting can trigger a biological process called autophagy, a sort of cellular spring cleaning. In longer fasts, for example 24–72 hours, there's evidence of new stem cell production, improved insulin sensitivity and even slowed biological aging.

In other words, going without food doesn't *weaken* you; it may renew you.

But in today's culture of constant convenience and consumption, the idea of being hungry even for a few hours seems radical. We've been conditioned to believe discomfort is something to avoid at all costs. But discomfort is where growth happens. Our modern lives are designed for comfort, yet our biology is designed for challenge. Fasting reconnects us to that truth.

Benefits of Fasting

- Boosts insulin sensitivity.
- Promotes cellular repair (autophagy).
- Increases growth hormone levels.
- Supports mental clarity and focus.
- May stimulate stem cell regeneration during extended fasts.
- Encourages a better relationship with food and body awareness.

How to Start Fasting (If You're New to It)

If you're new to fasting, take a gentle, informed approach. Here are some ways to ease in:

Fasting Tips:

- Start with a 12:12 fasting window (12 hours fasting, 12 hours eating).
- Gradually build up to 16:8 (16 hours fasting, 8-hour eating window).
- Drink plenty of water, herbal teas and electrolytes.
- Focus on nutrient-dense meals during your eating window.
- Break your fast gently with protein, healthy fats and fibre.
- Avoid processed or high-sugar foods during your eating window.
- Listen to your body; this is about balance, not punishment.

A Word of Caution

Fasting isn't for everyone.

If you're pregnant, breastfeeding, diabetic or navigating complex health conditions, consult a trusted health professional before attempting any form of intermittent or prolonged fasting. Women in perimenopause or menopause may find fasting affects their hormones differently, particularly if stress levels are already high. Always tailor your approach to your unique physiology and life stage.

Final Thought

Fasting is not about deprivation; it's about *liberation*. It's a chance to realign with your biology, reset your relationship with food and tap into a strength that's always been there.

You're not broken. You're just out of rhythm.

Fasting might be the beat that brings you back in tune.

Eating Out Without Selling Out

If dining out is a regular part of your lifestyle, having a strategy is essential. You can absolutely enjoy the social and cultural richness of eating out, without compromising your health goals or undoing all your good work.

Here are some grounded, realistic strategies to help you stay aligned when eating out:

- **Choose the venue wisely.** Whenever possible, suggest restaurants that offer clean, wholesome options. A little research ahead of time can go a long way.
- **You're in charge of your plate.** Just because others are ordering for the table doesn't mean you need to eat everything served. It's not rude to politely decline. Your body, your choice.
- **Scan smart.** Look for meals built around lean proteins, fresh

vegetables and whole-food ingredients. Choose tomato-based sauces over creamy ones, request dressings and condiments on the side, and don't be afraid to ask for swaps (for example, salad instead of chips, no bread). If dessert is calling your name, consider sharing or choosing a lighter option such as fresh fruit or a sorbet.

- **Be confident in your boundaries.** If you're fasting, don't be afraid to share that upfront. A simple, *I'm not eating right now but I'm here for the company*, is enough. People will respect your discipline far more than you think.
- **Drink with awareness.** Water is always the best choice with meals. If you're drinking alcohol, steer clear of sugary mixers and pace yourself mindfully. One or two thoughtfully chosen drinks is very different from drinking on autopilot.
- **Time your day around the occasion.** If you know you're heading out for a big meal, try to fast beforehand and prioritise hydration. This helps your body prepare and process the indulgence more easily.

The key message? Eating out should be enjoyable, not stressful, but it shouldn't be something you leave to chance if you're doing it often. With a few intentional habits and a mindset of conscious choice, you can navigate dining out without derailing your health.

That said, it's important to remember: you'll rarely know exactly what oils, preservatives, or ingredients are used in restaurant kitchens. That's why preparing your own food, at least most of the time, remains one of the most powerful health habits you can build. Like anything else in *Balanced Success*, it's not about perfection, it's about intention and balance.

Key Messages: Health & Vitality - Nutrition

- Health is the foundation of sustainable success, not a side goal.
- Prioritising nutrition boosts clarity, energy, mood and resilience.
- Telomeres are biological indicators of aging; lifestyle choices can slow their decline.
- A healthy gut is central to mental, emotional and physical performance.
- Whole, seasonal and local foods are key to long-term vitality.
- Glucose stability impacts energy, mood, hormones and inflammation.
- Fasting is a biologically natural reset, not deprivation.
- Eating out can be healthy with conscious choices and confidence.
- This is not about control or perfection; it's about aligned nourishment.

Balanced Success Check-In: Nutrition

How to Complete This Check-In

1. **Rate each area (1–10).**
   1 = off-track/struggling, 5 = mixed/variable, 10 = thriving/consistent.

2. **Add quick notes.**
   In "Notes or Reflections", capture wins, friction points, patterns, triggers or context (e.g. travel, deadlines).

3. **Choose one tiny upgrade.**
   Pick **one** specific, low-effort change for the next seven days. Aim to "make the good choice the easy choice".

Balanced Success Check In: Nutrition

Area	Score (1-10)	Notes/Reflections
Whole-Foods Ratio		
Protein & Fibre Balance		
Plant Diversity (aim 30+/wk)		
Hydration		
Glucose-Stability Habits (veggies first / post-meal walk)		

 Reflection Prompt: *What's one small change I could make this week to make the good choice the easy choice?*

Health & Vitality: Sleep & Relaxation

I didn't truly understand the importance of sleep until after I had my second child. Let's just say…she wasn't the best sleeper. And for the first year of her life, I operated like a zombie.

I had just turned 40. I was juggling part-time work in my own business, raising two children and managing a household. My limits were being pushed from every angle.

I was continually exhausted, felt adrenal fatigue in every part of my being, my emotions were on the edge and my brain constantly felt it was working through a fog.

One day, everything came crashing down. I became convinced that someone had stolen our house keys and that someone was watching us. I spiralled. Paranoia set in. And in that moment, I completely broke down. But it wasn't just me that crumbled. I brought my whole family into the storm.

Long story short—the keys were found. We were safe. But I wasn't. That breakdown was the wake-up call. Sleep wasn't a luxury. It was non-negotiable.

Consistent, high-quality sleep isn't an extravagance; it's essential. The old success paradigm glorified late nights and relentless hours, wearing sleep deprivation as a badge of honour. But in today's world, sacrificing rest is no longer a mark of dedication; it's a sign of imbalance. According to sleepfoundation.org, chronic sleep loss not only undermines health but also impairs decision-making, emotional regulation and overall performance.

Over the next five years, it is likely you will be pushed to your limits in many ways. Facing an unchartered and treacherous terrain with the changes associated with changes such as AI will no doubt result in accelerated stress, fatigue and feeling overwhelmed.

In fact, there is actually a term now used to describe this specific type of stress. As AI continues to reshape our work environments, many leaders are facing a rising but often silent burden: technostress. This refers to the psychological strain that arises when we feel overwhelmed by rapid technological change. For executives navigating constant innovation, evolving platforms and fears around redundancy or irrelevance, this pressure is real. And it's not just about learning new systems; it's about managing the emotional load of staying ahead. Sleep plays a crucial role here.

The Data Is In: Leaders Who Don't Sleep Make Worse Decisions

Research published in Harvard Business Review (Van Dam & van der Helm, 2016) found that 43% of leaders report not getting enough sleep at least four nights a week. The effects? Reduced focus, poorer judgment, diminished creativity and a sharp decline in emotional intelligence; all the core attributes that define effective leadership.

Leaders running on sleep debt are more likely to misread situations, respond impulsively and struggle with strategic thinking. In contrast, those who prioritise quality sleep are better equipped to lead with clarity, empathy and vision.

BALANCED SUCCESS

It's a simple but powerful truth: your leadership effectiveness is directly influenced by how well you sleep.

In high-stakes environments, particularly during disruptive times like this AI-driven era, sleep becomes one of the smartest investments a leader can make.

Think of sleep as your brain's nightly cleanse. According to sleepopolis.com, just as you shower to maintain physical hygiene, sleep clears out mental clutter, flushing toxins, consolidating memories and preparing you for the day ahead. Simultaneously, your body undergoes vital repairs; cells regenerate, the immune system strengthens and hormonal balances are restored.

For most adults, 7–9 hours of uninterrupted rest each night is ideal. Quality sleep means falling asleep within 30 minutes, minimal awakenings and waking up feeling refreshed.

Compelling Reasons to Prioritise Sleep

- **Enhanced Cognitive Function**: Improves memory, attention and decision-making. Sleep-deprived individuals are more error-prone and impulsive.
- **Emotional Well-being**: Regulates emotions, reducing stress, anxiety and mood swings.
- **Physical Health**: Supports heart health, immune function and healthy weight.
- **Hormonal Balance**: Regulates appetite, growth and stress hormones.

Occasional late nights happen. But when sleeplessness becomes a habit, it disrupts your health equilibrium. Prioritizing sleep isn't about perfection; it's about honouring its foundational role in your energy and alignment.

Sleep Optimisation Strategies (inspired by Dr. Andrew Huberman & Amanda Slinger)

- Maintain a cool room: ~18°C (65°F).
- Consistent sleep/wake schedule.
- Dim lights in the evening; switch to red/amber lighting.
- Limit screen time one hour before bed.
- Avoid eating 2–3 hours before sleep.
- Limit caffeine after 2–4pm; avoid alcohol close to bed.
- Calm pre-sleep rituals: reading, breathwork, stretching.
- Reserve bed for sleep and intimacy only.

The Truth About Early Birds and Night Owls

Not everyone is wired to rise early. Chronotype, your natural sleep-wake rhythm, is genetic and linked to human evolution. In ancestral times, some stayed up late to guard the tribe; others rose early to lead the day. This diversity remains coded in us.

National Institutes of Health (NIH) research confirms: being a night owl isn't a flaw, it's biology. The key is aligning your rest patterns with your body's natural rhythm whenever possible.

Relaxation: The Art of Conscious Restoration

While sleep regenerates passively, relaxation is a conscious opportunity to reset. It activates the parasympathetic nervous system, lowers stress hormones and brings clarity. According to AdventHealth (2023) and the University of Sydney (2021), regular relaxation improves health, resilience and sleep quality.

Benefits of Regular Relaxation

- Enhanced mental clarity.
- Lower blood pressure and muscle tension.
- Boosted immunity.
- Improved emotional regulation and sleep.

Simple Daily Relaxation Tools

- Deep breathing (4-7-8, box breathing).
- Progressive muscle relaxation.
- Mindfulness meditation (5–10 minutes).
- Nature walks without headphones.
- Creative flow: journaling, music, mindful cooking.

Reflection Prompt: Reclaiming Rest

- When was the last time I allowed myself to do nothing without guilt?
- What does relaxation currently look like for me?
- Have I ignored signs of burnout to push through?
- What simple rituals would help me feel grounded and rested?
- Relaxation isn't indulgence. It's intelligence. It's wisdom in action.

 Key Messages: Health & Vitality: Sleep & Relaxation

- Sleep fuels emotional resilience, decision-making and leadership clarity.
- The AI era increases stress; sleep is your defence and anchor.
- Relaxation is conscious, intentional restoration that rewires your nervous system.
- Respect your body's unique rhythm and create rituals for both rest and sleep.
- Small, consistent practices offer big results in clarity, calm and wellbeing.

How to Complete This Check-In

1. **Rate each area (1–10).**
   1 = off-track/struggling, 5 = mixed/variable, 10 = thriving/consistent.

2. **Add quick notes.**
   In "Notes or Reflections", capture wins, friction points, patterns, triggers, or context (e.g. travel, deadlines).

3. **Choose one tiny upgrade.**
   Pick **one** specific, low-effort change for the next seven days. Aim to "make the good choice the easy choice".

Balanced Success Check In: Sleep & Relaxation

Area	Score (1-10)	Notes/Reflections
Sleep Consistency		
Sleep Quality		
Daily Relaxation Rituals		
Stress Regulation		
Respecting Your Chronotype		

Reflection Prompt: *What's one small change I could make this week to protect my rest time like a vital meeting?*

Health & Vitality: Exercise

Exercise is a must for anyone who wants to live a full, vibrant life built on energy, strength and mental clarity.

For leaders in particular, movement is one of the fastest ways to release tension, shift emotional states and prime your mind for the day ahead. It resets your nervous system, recharges your mental focus, and anchors you in your body—something many high performers forget until burnout sets in.

We often associate exercise with weight loss or body image. But its true power lies far deeper.

Moving your body most days isn't just about aesthetics; it's about building the capacity to lead powerfully, adapt resiliently and live well for the long game.

I've made a lifelong commitment to exercise at least five days a week. And I'll be honest, that's not always easy. Like many of you, I juggle competing priorities: two young daughters, a growing business and a full calendar. But one thing has never changed and that is my values. Vitality sits at the top of my personal compass, second only to love. Movement isn't a to-do list item. It's a core expression of who I am.

So when I'm faced with choices—an early meeting, a client lunch, an invitation to skip the gym—I filter them through that value. Not from guilt or pressure, but from alignment. When I move, I feel more grounded, more energised and more present. That's how I know I'm leading from integrity.

Debunking the Weight Loss Myth

While movement supports fat loss, it's far more effective for weight maintenance, metabolic regulation and psychological wellbeing.

In *Burn: The Misunderstood Science of Metabolism* (Pontzer, 2022), Dr. Herman Pontzer reveals that the human body adapts to increased activity by reducing energy expenditure elsewhere. In other words, we can't out-train a poor diet or high-stress lifestyle. Neuroscientist Dr. Andrew Huberman adds that exercise acts as a neural signal, telling the brain and body to adapt, recalibrate and thrive.

The Real Benefits of Exercise

- **Flushes toxins and supports recovery**: Movement enhances circulation and lymphatic drainage, clearing waste and restoring equilibrium.
- **Improves cognitive function**: Aerobic exercise increases brain-derived neurotrophic factor (BDNF), a key protein for memory, learning, and brain plasticity. Studies from *Harvard Health* (Solan, 2024) show reduced dementia risk with consistent cardio.
- **Regulates hormones**: Exercise balances cortisol, improves insulin sensitivity, and boosts growth hormone—essential for energy, mood and metabolism.
- **Enhances brain chemistry**: Just 20 minutes of moderate exercise

can spike dopamine and serotonin, lifting mood and focus naturally (*JAMA Psychiatry*, 2023).
- **Strengthens immune response**: Moderate movement decreases chronic inflammation and enhances the body's ability to fend off illness.
- **Improves sleep quality**: Regular exercise aligns circadian rhythm and supports deep, restorative sleep cycles (*Sleep Medicine Reviews*, 2022).
- **Drives habit change**: Movement triggers a cascade of better decisions, including healthier food choices, more hydration and improved boundaries.
- **Builds emotional resilience**: Exercise is stress rehearsal. It trains your nervous system to stay calm under physical and mental load.
- **Supports longevity**: Strength training preserves bone density and muscle mass, which is critical as we age.
- **Improves relationships**: When you feel good in your body, you show up more connected, patient and engaged at work and home.

Consistency Over Intensity: Make it Work for You

Consistency beats perfection. Don't chase intensity or comparison, chase sustainability. Your training should evolve with your season of life.

Here are six science-backed strategies to stay consistent:
1. **Schedule movement like a meeting**: Protect it like you would with your most valuable client.
2. **Break it into blocks**: 10 minutes here, 20 there; it all adds up.
3. **Weekend advantage**: Use flexible time to recharge with movement.
4. **Long-game mindset**: Don't train for events, train for life.
5. **Visible accountability**: Track your movement. Visibility reinforces identity.
6. **Design over motivation**: Prepare your gear, set your time and lower friction to start.

The Identity Shift That Makes It Stick

When exercise becomes who you are, not just what you do, everything changes. Your default becomes action. You override excuses. You embody a version of yourself that leads from vitality.

Take two people:
- *Person A* says, *I'm trying to work out more*. They see movement as an external task that is optional and often negotiable.
- *Person B* says, *I don't skip workouts, it's just who I am*. Their identity is rooted in consistency. They plan ahead, adapt when schedules change and prioritise movement like brushing their teeth.

One operates from motivation. The other from identity.

Relying on motivation is a flawed strategy. Our brains are wired to conserve energy, which means we subconsciously seek comfort and avoid exertion. Most of us won't *feel* like exercising, especially when we're tired, stressed or overwhelmed.
- "I've had a hard day, I deserve to rest."
- "Something more important has come up."
- "I just don't feel like it today."
- "It won't matter if I skip, I'll catch up next week."

But it *does* matter.

Every small decision compounds over time. Missing one workout isn't the problem; letting inconsistency become your new normal is.

A few hacks to prevent self-sabotage:

- Get your workout clothes ready the night before or keep them in your car.
- Write a sticky note: *No excuses; honour your energy.*
- Just put your workout clothes on and start.
- Visualise your future self and the life you're building.

Your identity is shaped by what you consistently do. When you act in alignment with who you want to become, the excuses lose power.

Refer to the habit section in Chapter Six which shows how to build a personal system that makes movement automatic.

Tanya's Reflection: From Athlete to Motherhood

After spending a decade training most days and competing every weekend, I found it difficult to return to everyday life. In my late teenage years, I outgrew my identity as a high-achieving athlete. I had other interests and commitments, and I had to come to terms with the fact that it no longer served where I was in my life.

Redefining my relationship with exercise wasn't easy. The effect was much deeper than I realised at the time: I lost my confidence, purpose, routine and courage. Also, something unexpected happened that hit me hard: I lost the very thing that kept my Dad and I connected on a special level. The time we spent together dropped away and suddenly, we had less to talk about.

Once I started studying Sports Science at university, things began to turn around. I finally found my tribe. I developed a passion for working out in the gym and joined a wide variety of group fitness classes. I loved being around other people who enjoyed exercise as much as I did.

I would still push the boundaries at times, training twice a day on occasion or overtraining for an adventure race. My brain was wired that way from a young age and it was difficult to change. I soon discovered the need to recalibrate the hard way, when injuries, exhaustion and a lack of balance caught up with me.

Many years on, after having two children and building a business, my relationship with exercise has changed. It's no longer about personal bests or big races. It's about longevity, mental clarity and emotional stability.

I still move most days, but now it looks like a spin class, a short strength session or a walk through the bush with my kids. The intensity has softened, but the meaning has deepened. I'm no longer chasing performance. I'm honouring my energy.

Because real strength isn't about how hard you push; it's about how consistently you show up, in all seasons, from a place of alignment.

Movement isn't a luxury. It's the foundation of leadership and life.

Key Messages: Health & Vitality: Exercise

- Exercise is a foundational investment in long-term health, energy and leadership capacity.
- It delivers benefits far beyond weight loss, including stress relief, brain function, sleep, emotional resilience and immune strength.
- Consistency matters more than intensity. Build habits that fit your season of life.
- Leaders who prioritise movement show up clearer, stronger and more connected, at home and at work.
- Identity matters: when movement becomes part of who you are, consistency follows naturally.

Balanced Success Check-In: Exercise

How to Complete This Check-In

1. **Rate each area (1–10).**
   1 = off-track/struggling, 5 = mixed/variable, 10 = thriving/consistent.

2. **Add quick notes.**
      In "Notes or Reflections", capture wins, friction points, patterns, triggers, or context (e.g. travel, deadlines).
   3. **Choose one tiny upgrade.**
      Pick **one** specific, low-effort change for the next seven days. Aim to "make the good choice the easy choice".

- **Physical Vitality:**
- **Energy for Leadership:**
- **Exercise Consistency:**
- **Movement Enjoyment:**

What's one small shift you can make this week to realign with your movement goals?

Remember: When your body is strong, your mind becomes unstoppable.

Eliminating Toxins

We live in a world where toxins are everywhere, hidden in our air, water, skincare and even household dust. Before diving into your personal experience and practical tips, let's highlight important insights from Dr Yvonne Burkart's conversation with Steven Bartlett on *The Diary of a CEO* podcast (2024). As a PhD toxicologist, she sounded a wakeup call for anyone serious about their health and leadership potential.

Key Takeaways from Dr Burkart:

- **"Fragrance" is often a code for hundreds of undisclosed chemicals**: These can include phthalates and endocrine disruptors that have been linked to fertility issues, developmental delays and serious illness.
- **Tap water isn't as clean as you think**: Microplastics,

endocrine disruptors and PFAS ("forever chemicals") are common in unfiltered water. She urged switching to wholehouse or pointofuse filtration systems.
- **Dust accumulates toxins**: Indoor air pollution can be just as harmful as outdoor smog. Dust often holds heavy metals, ozone byproducts and microplastics. Regularly dusting with damp cloths and using air purifiers can help.
- **Beauty and haircare carry hidden risks**: Many personal care items contain parabens, phthalates and other endocrine disruptors. Dr Burkart recommends choosing products labelled "phthalatefree", "parabenfree", and avoiding vague terms like "fragrance."
- **Perfume isn't just air freshener, it can be a toxin delivery system**: These aren't limited to candles; any product listing "perfume" or "fragrance" may emit volatile organic compounds (VOCs) that derange hormonal systems over time.

Tanya's Tips on Toxins

We are not taught this stuff, and the system in place is not there to protect your health. It's built to generate profit. So, it's up to *you* to take responsibility and make more informed decisions. The research is there; it's just not in front of your face.

When I first discovered the impact that poisonous toxins have on our bodies, I scanned my home environment and was shocked with what I found:
- I had been cooking with non-stick pans and plastic utensils. When heated, these leach toxins directly into the food.
- I had placed candles throughout my house with "parfum" as an ingredient, releasing VOCs into the air that my family was breathing.
- My skincare and makeup were full of chemicals. When you realise our skin is our largest organ, it's terrifying to consider what I had

been applying for decades.
- We were drinking unfiltered water from the tap that was full of parasites and toxins.
- I was using cleaning and laundry products that were full of nasty chemicals.

The Hidden Plastic Problem

Consider this: you buy a bottle of water from the shop, something so common it hardly registers. But that plastic bottle has already begun leaching microplastics into the water, especially if it's been exposed to heat (such as sitting in a hot car or warehouse).

At the supermarket, most food is wrapped in plastic. We don't think twice, but these plastics transfer directly to our food. When plastic is heated, the transfer rate of toxins is significantly higher. According to recent research published in *Environmental Science & Technology*, microplastics are now found in human blood, lungs, placentas and even breastmilk. Once these plastic particles are in the body, they don't simply leave, they accumulate.

The Hidden Hormonal Threat: Endocrine Disruptors

Many of the toxins we've mentioned, like phthalates, parabens, PFAS, and synthetic fragrances, fall into a category known as endocrine-disrupting chemicals (EDCs). These substances interfere with the body's hormonal systems, often mimicking or blocking natural hormones such as estrogen, testosterone and thyroid hormones. The result?

Profound disruption to everything from metabolism and sleep to fertility, cognitive function and emotional regulation.

A landmark report by the World Health Organisation and the United Nations Environment Programme classified EDCs as a global threat to human health and linked them to developmental disorders, hormone-related cancers, obesity, diabetes and reproductive issues.

What's more troubling is that even low-level exposure can have lasting effects, especially when exposure occurs over time or during sensitive life stages like pregnancy
and childhood.

For leaders, the impact is more subtle but still damaging. Brain fog, burnout, mood swings, disrupted sleep and lowered vitality can all be downstream effects of these invisible disruptors. As Dr. Burkart emphasised in her interview, *You can't lead at your best when your biochemistry is under attack.*

That's why eliminating toxins isn't about perfection; it's about protecting your internal equilibrium so you can lead with clarity, confidence and capacity.

A Simple Toxin-Elimination Plan

Toxin Source	What to Watch	First Action Step
Tap Water	PFAS, chlorine, microplastics	Add a certified filter to your kitchen tap (e.g. activated carbon + reverse osmosis)
Dust & Indoor Air	VOCs, microplastics, heavy metals	Use a HEPA air purifier, dust with damp cloth weekly
"Fragrance" Products	Endocrine disruptors, VOCs	Replace with fragrance-free or fully disclosed ingredient products
Skincare / Haircare	Parabens, phthalates, hidden dyes	Choose certified "clean" beauty and natural alternatives
Plastics in Food	Microplastics, endocrine disruptors	Store food in glass/stainless containers, avoid heating food in plastic
Cookware	PFAS, PTFE from non-stick pans	Switch to stainless steel, cast iron, or ceramic pans

Why it Matters

Toxin overload quietly erodes clarity, energy and resilience…the very foundations of leadership. Unknown chemicals accumulate and impair mental focus, mood stability, immune function, sleep quality and even long-term health. When you're regularly exposed, recovery becomes harder and pathways to vitality close off.

That's why eliminating common toxins isn't just health optimization, it's a strategic leadership choice. It's a step toward preserving your mental wealth, buffer capacity and the ability to show up fully, for yourself and those you lead.

The Leadership Impact

When you clear toxins, you support your body's innate detox systems—liver, kidneys, lymph, nervous system and brain function. That translates into:
- **Sharper clarity**—no more fog or sporadic energy dips.
- **Balanced emotions**—less irritability or reactive moods.
- **Consistent energy**—even on demanding days.
- **Resilience**—a body that recovers faster, a mind that adapts quicker.
- **Longevity**—you protect the body and brain you need to lead well for decades.

Final Thought

As Dr Burkart shared, *Even small changes can have a big impact over time.* That's the *Balanced Success* way; choose micro-steps now for macro-legacy later.

Your body is your headquarters. When its environment is clear, you think clearer, lead stronger and navigate the storms smarter. Let's give it the best chance.

 Key Messages: Health & Vitality: Eliminating Toxins

- Toxins are found in everyday items like water, air, food and personal care products.
- Microplastics and endocrine disruptors (EDCs) are especially concerning as they stay in the body and interfere with hormones.

BALANCED SUCCESS

- Making small, consistent changes (e.g. using clean products, filtering water, changing cookware) protects long-term health and leadership performance.
- Eliminating toxins isn't about perfection; it's about leadership clarity and vitality.

Balanced Success Check-In: Eliminating Toxins

How to Complete This Check-In

1. **Rate each area (1–10).**
   1 = off-track/struggling, 5 = mixed/variable, 10 = thriving/consistent.
2. **Add quick notes.**
   In "Notes or Reflections", capture wins, friction points, patterns, triggers, or context (e.g., travel, deadlines).
3. **Choose one tiny upgrade.**
   Pick **one** specific, low-effort change for the next seven days. Aim to "make the good choice the easy choice".

Balanced Success Check In: Eliminating Toxins

Area	Score (1-10)	Notes/Reflections
Home & Cleaning Products (low-tox swaps)		
Water, Cookware & Food Contact (filter; glass/steel; avoid heating plastics)		
Personal Care & Fragrance (simpler ingredients; unscented)		
Air Quality, Ventilation & Mould (open windows/HEPA/extract fans)		
Plastics & Microplastics Reduction (cut single-use; mindful of synthetics)		

Reflection Prompt: *What's one small swap I'll make this week to lower everyday exposure at home or work?*

A final note: Vitality is your inner power source

In this section, we've explored how your body is your greatest asset, not a machine to be pushed, numbed or manipulated.

The truth is, vitality is the energy that fuels clarity, leadership, emotional regulation and joy. It's not about chasing perfection or obsessing over trends. It's about remembering that your body is always speaking to you.

The question is: *Are you listening?*

You don't need to overhaul everything. Start where you are. Choose one habit that aligns with the future version of you, the one who feels strong, clear and aligned with integrity about what matters most. Let the momentum build from there.

Because vitality doesn't come from doing more. It comes from coming back to yourself.

You deserve to feel good…not just sometimes, but consistently. Let health be the foundation that allows you to lead with strength, live with presence and love with your whole heart.

Your future self is counting on you.

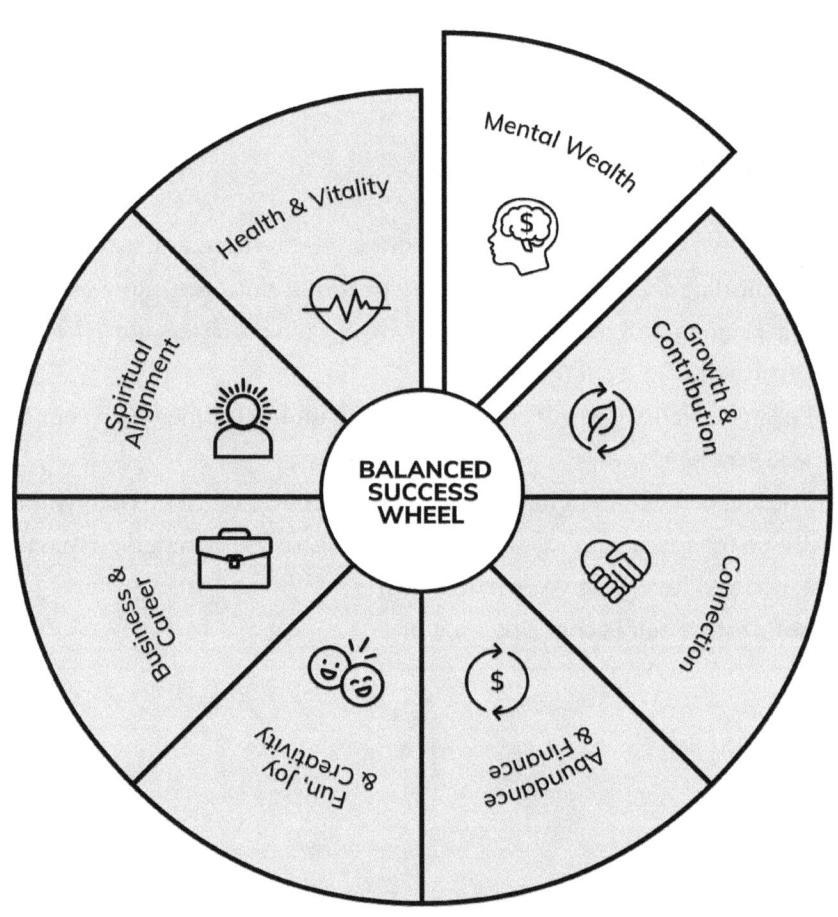

CHAPTER SIX

Mental Wealth

I f *Balanced Success* is the destination of your plane, then *Mental Wealth* is the fuel that gets you there.

Mental Wealth means looking after yourself in a proactive, well-rounded and consistent way. When you're healthy, happy and fulfilled, your mind becomes the optimal environment for doing your best work, not just in your business, but in your relationships, your health and your leadership.

According to neuroscientist Prof. Isaac Prilleltensky and policy research from the Institute for Mental Wealth (University of Birmingham), mental wealth is more than just the absence of illness; it's a socioeconomic asset. One that enhances innovation, productivity and human potential, particularly during times of rapid change.

That might sound obvious. But in high-pressure environments, even the obvious gets overlooked. When cognitive depletion creeps in, and it will, our ability to care for ourselves drops to the bottom of the list. Add the endless to-dos of modern life, and before long, you're running on empty.

I can already hear the objections:

But I do some things for myself. I'm not that bad. I'm doing the best I can, I'm not superhuman. Sure, I have ups and downs, but I'm doing better than most of my peers.

Here's the uncomfortable truth: If you're consistently neglecting one or more of the components that make up your mental wealth, it *will* catch up with you. Maybe not today.

Maybe not this year. But over time, the cost doesn't just increase, it compounds. That means the longer you delay, the *faster* the consequences escalate.

Life catches up, and fast.

So What Exactly is Mental Wealth?

Let's break it down.

Mental refers to the mind, or our thoughts, emotions, clarity and inner processing.

Wealth is commonly associated with money or valuable assets. But if we go deeper, the Cambridge Dictionary offers a second definition: *a large amount of something good.*

That definition carries a completely different energy.

Mental Wealth, then, is the mind's ability to produce *a large amount of good*, in terms of creativity, emotional intelligence, clear decision-making, resilience, presence and purpose.

Our minds are powerful. But like any powerful engine, they require care, fuel and regular tune-ups. If we want to live a life filled with good things, connection, vitality, joy, we must create the mental conditions for those things to grow. And that starts with how we treat ourselves daily.

So why is the examination and discussion of the mind still taboo in many areas of society?

Because we can't see it. A bruised toe gets sympathy. Limping into school in a moon boot sparks instant concern. But when someone's struggling mentally, when they withdraw, seem "off" or less engaged, the reaction is often confusion, avoidance or judgment.

We don't know what to say. We don't understand what's happening. And truthfully, neither might the person going through it.

Mental health isn't like a broken toe. You can't strap it up and carry on as usual. Our inner world is complex, layered and deeply individual. That's why mental wealth is so important; it's the proactive side of mental health. It's not waiting for things to break before we act. It's investing now so the cracks never become fractures.

Take John. A high-performing executive, father and gym-goer. From the outside, he seems in control. But beneath the success lies unresolved trauma from a difficult childhood. He's done everything he can to be a great provider and father, yet he's never made space to process his past. He locked his pain away years ago. But unprocessed emotions don't disappear; they wait.

Despite appearing high-functioning, the cracks begin to show. Eventually, John is diagnosed with depression. He tries to power through, but the waves keep crashing, harder each time. These waves aren't just symptoms; they're soul signals. It's not about erasing the past. It's about *releasing* it. Without that inner work, no amount of success will fill the void.

Now meet Jill. A small business owner, emotionally intelligent and driven. She's used to prioritising her health, through meal prepping and early workouts, and she has a vibrant energy. But over the past few years, work and family demands have pulled her in every direction but inward. She's now six kilograms above her usual weight and barely recognizes herself in the mirror.

Her zest fades. Her confidence drops. Her business feels heavier. She disengages from her family, not out of love lost, but because she's running on fumes. Jill didn't fail. She just forgot to put herself on the list.

The Rising Relevance of Mental Wealth

The definition of *mental health* traditionally focuses on the condition of one's mind and the presence or absence of mental illness. But that's no longer enough. We are on the edge of a global shift, technological, economic, social and the prevalence of mental health challenges is projected to rise dramatically.

Technology is evolving daily, hourly even, and Artificial Intelligence is just one factor that will change the way we live and work. With that will come uncertainty, role redundancy and existential anxiety for many. Fear, disconnection and overwhelm are already increasing, and the pace of the world is only accelerating.

Which is why now, more than ever, *mental health* must become a priority.

Purpose: The Quiet Power Behind a Fulfilled Life

Purpose is a word that's become so overused it's easy to ignore. In boardrooms, business books and social media reels, it often shows up as a buzzword, not a deeply lived truth. We get more excited by what's trending: AI breakthroughs, political debates, ice baths, hacks for high performance. But purpose? That feels…slow. Abstract. Optional.

And yet, it's everything.

We are human beings, not human doings, yet most people spend their lives in the doing phase. We wake up, dive into our calendars, tick off to-dos, respond to demands and push through until we collapse into bed. Then repeat. What we rarely do is pause long enough to ask the bigger questions:

Why am I doing this?

Is this aligned with what actually matters to me?
Is this success…or is it just motion?
What would a meaningful life really look like?

Because without those questions, it's easy to get stuck in autopilot. Busy. Productive. Externally successful. But internally? Numb. Disconnected. Off course.

That's how a decade passes in a blur. And suddenly you're asking: *How did I get here?*

What Is Purpose, Really?

Purpose isn't just about saving the world or launching a non-profit organisation. It's not something reserved for the chosen few with a calling so obvious it's written in the stars.

Purpose is simply your *why*. It's the inner clarity that gives meaning to your life.

Purpose is the thread that weaves your work, your relationships and your choices into something coherent, something that feels true. When you're connected to it, you feel anchored, alive and resilient. You know what matters and why it matters. That doesn't mean life becomes easy. It just means you have a compass.

And for leaders, that compass is invaluable.

Purpose fuels clarity in decisions, resilience in uncertainty, and alignment in the way you lead your team, your clients and your life.

Purpose can be bold and public, leading a movement, writing a book, starting a mission-led business. Or it can be quiet and deeply personal, raising emotionally healthy children, being a safe place for others, healing a family lineage. Both are equally powerful.

What matters is that your life feels meaningful to you.

And that meaning is self-generated. You can't download it from a podcast. You can't borrow it from your partner. And you can't find it by chasing someone else's version of success.

Your purpose lives at the intersection of three things:
- What lights you up.
- What challenges you to grow.
- What contributes to others in some way.

It evolves over time. What felt purposeful in your 20s may not feel the same in your 40s. And that's okay. Purpose isn't fixed, it's fluid. But it requires something most people avoid: time spent listening inward.

Because purpose doesn't shout. It whispers. And to hear it, you must slow down long enough to listen.

Purpose is one of the deepest roots in your *Balanced Success* foundation. It's not the loudest, but without it, the whole tree leans.

The Cost of Living Without Purpose

Living without a sense of purpose doesn't always look like failure. In fact, it often looks like success, from the outside.

You're ticking boxes. Meeting deadlines. Running a business. Earning the income. Raising the kids. Posting the photos. But underneath it all, there's a quiet sense of disconnection. A hum of, *is this it?* that never quite goes away.

Here's the truth: A lack of purpose doesn't always scream. It erodes slowly, in the form of burnout, overworking, emotional numbing, overconsumption, scrolling, drinking, striving, comparing. It's not always obvious until you hit a breaking point.

And that breaking point usually shows up as one of three things:

- **Exhaustion** — where your energy is always drained, no matter how much you rest.
- **Disillusionment** — where the things you once chased no longer feel satisfying.
- **Escapism** — where you constantly look for ways to avoid being present in your own life.

Without purpose, people become more reactive. They chase success without ever defining it. They say yes to everything because they don't know what truly matters. They numb discomfort instead of listening to what it's trying to say.

And eventually, they wake up one day, in a job, a relationship, a life, that doesn't feel like theirs.

This is the hidden cost of living without alignment. Not just the missed opportunities, but the internal regret of knowing you were meant for more and didn't make time to ask what that "more" was.

Reconnecting With Purpose

You don't find purpose by thinking harder. You uncover it by paying attention.

Purpose isn't always a grand mission or life-changing event. Sometimes, it's subtle; a pull, a whisper, a spark that says, *this matters*. It's less about what you do and more about how you feel when you do it.

Here are five ways to start reconnecting:

1. **Notice What Lights You Up**
    a. What are the moments when you lose track of time?
    b. What topics or activities energise you, even if they don't "make sense" right now?
    c. That spark is a clue.

Prompt: When was the last time I felt fully alive? What was I doing, and why did it feel so meaningful?

2. Reflect on Your Pain

   a. Often, purpose is born from pain. The things that hurt you, broke you or shaped you often hold the seeds of what you're here to heal or help in others.
   b. Purpose doesn't always come from passion. Sometimes, it comes from what you've overcome.

Prompt: What have I been through that changed me? What would I tell someone else going through the same thing?

3. Revisit Your Younger Self

   a. Before the world told you what was realistic, you had dreams. Go back to that version of you.
   b. What did they love? What did they believe in? What did they know before they were told to be practical?

Prompt: What did I want to be or do before I started filtering myself? What's still true about that?

4. Clarify Your Impact

   a. Purpose is often found at the intersection of what you're good at, what you care about and who you want to serve.
   b. It doesn't have to be your job, but it does need to feel meaningful.

Prompt: If I could help one type of person or solve one problem in the world, what would it be?

5. Experiment, Don't Overthink

   a. Purpose evolves. You don't need to have the perfect answer.
   b. Try new things. Follow your curiosity.

> Pay attention to what feels right. Purpose grows when you're in motion.

Prompt: What's one thing I can try this month that feels aligned, even if it scares me?

> *"The meaning of life is to find your gift.*
> *The purpose of life is to give it away."*
> **— Pablo Picasso**

Tanya's Soul-Level Fulfilment: Coming Home to Myself

I spent most of my 30s feeling lost and empty. From a business perspective, I was dedicated and driven, but deep inside there was a void; a quiet, aching hollowness that no amount of success could fill. The more I ignored it, the darker it became. On paper, everything looked great. But the truth was, my life was missing something essential.

Somewhere along the way, I had forgotten who I was. I had left my soul behind. I couldn't remember what made me light up, what made my heart sing. So I filled the gap with what other people wanted from me. I kept saying yes. I kept performing. I ignored the signs, and there were many, that something was off. I pushed through and refused to quit.

It wasn't until COVID hit and I moved back to Australia that I finally slowed down enough to listen. That season of forced stillness gave me the space to turn inward. At first, it was unfamiliar and confronting. But little by little, I began to ask myself deeper questions. I peeled back the layers I'd built to survive and underneath, I found my soul again.

From that place, I began creating a new kind of life. One where success wasn't defined by external outcomes, but by internal alignment. One where I could finally feel fulfilled, not because I'd achieved something, but because I was becoming someone I actually wanted to be.

That's the difference between chasing success and living with purpose.

Soul-level fulfillment is quiet, but powerful. It doesn't come from accolades, milestones or checking boxes. It comes from knowing you

BALANCED SUCCESS

are living in alignment with what matters most. To you. It's a feeling of wholeness that grows when your outer world starts to reflect the truth of your inner world.

This kind of purpose doesn't demand the spotlight. It whispers. It guides. It brings peace, not pressure. And once you've felt it, you'll never want to live any other way.

Because the ultimate success isn't what you built; it's who you became along the way.

Purpose is more than a buzzword. It's your internal compass, guiding your energy, decisions and sense of fulfillment.

Key Messages: Mental Wealth: Purpose

- Living without purpose often leads to chronic dissatisfaction, burnout and a sense of disconnection, even when life looks "successful" from the outside.
- Soul-level fulfillment comes from aligning your actions with what matters most to you, not just following external expectations.
- Purpose can evolve over time, but it must be intentional. It requires reflection, honesty and the courage to go inward.
- Your leadership, clarity and sense of meaning are all amplified when you live and work from a place of alignment.

Balanced Success Check-In: Purpose

How to Complete This Check-In

1. **Rate each area (1–10).**
   1 = off-track/struggling, 5 = mixed/variable, 10 = thriving/consistent.
2. **Add quick notes.**
   In "Notes or Reflections", capture wins, friction points, patterns, triggers, or context (e.g. travel, deadlines).
3. **Choose one tiny upgrade.**
   Pick **one** specific, low-effort change for the next seven days.

- Clarity of my purpose: ____
- Daily actions match my values: ____
- My work feels meaningful: ____
- I feel I am contributing beyond myself: ____
- I protect time for purpose work: ____
- I have clear goals linked to my purpose: ____
- I make brave choices that honour my purpose: ____
- My relationships support my purpose: ____

- I feel energised by how I spend my time: ____
- I am making steady progress: ____

One Small Shift: *What's one small step you can take this week to reconnect with what really matters?*

Mental Wealth: Core Life Values

There's an invisible compass shaping your life, quietly, constantly and often without your awareness. It's called your set of core values. And in the busyness of life, we rarely stop to define them.

One of the most powerful exercises I've ever done was uncovering my core values.

Now I know what you might be thinking: *Values work? I've seen this before. Not again.*

But trust me, don't skip this section of the chapter.

This isn't about ticking a personal development box. This is about identifying the invisible operating system guiding every decision you make, consciously or not.

If you give this section your time and presence, it has the potential to reshape your life in a deeply transformational way. Let me show you why.

Why Values Matter More Than You Think

Core values aren't just words on a page. They are emotional anchors. They influence the way we think, act, react, prioritise and lead. They form the internal compass that points us toward fulfilment or misalignment.

Think about it: You probably know your company's values or could at least find them on a poster in the tea-room, or a folder in H: drive. But do you know your own? And do you know how to find them?

> It's ironic how easily we can recite the values of a business, yet struggle to articulate the values guiding our own lives.

And yet, they're there, shaping every moment, every choice. The challenge isn't that we don't have values, it's that we haven't consciously named them.

Where Do Core Values Come From?

Our core values are formed early, between the ages of two and seven, through a mix of emotional experiences, environmental cues, culture and relationships. They're not chosen; they're absorbed.

In psychological terms, they form part of our schema, the mental shortcuts that influence how we interpret and respond to life.

We experience something, we feel something and we unconsciously make meaning of it. Over time, repeated emotional patterns solidify into what becomes a core value.

For example:
- A child who grows up in a chaotic home may unconsciously develop a deep value for peace or safety.
- A child who receives love only when they succeed may value achievement or recognition.

This means our values are highly individual and deeply tied to emotion.

How Values Shape Our Everyday Lives

Every single day, you make thousands of decisions, what to do with your time, energy, focus, attention. Most of them happen automatically.

Now imagine if the unseen filter driving those decisions isn't aligned with the life you want to create.

That's why identifying your core values is so crucial. They reveal your decision-making logic. And when values conflict, the ones ranked higher will always win.

Let's say one of your top values is love for your family, but you've unconsciously prioritised achievement above it. You'll continue to overwork, even when you say family matters most, because your behaviour follows the hierarchy of your values, not your stated intentions.

Tanya's Tips on Establishing and Living Core Values

To make this practical, I want to share how my own top values show up in daily life, because values aren't just words, they're lived.

1. **Love** – Deep connection with myself and others. This shows up in how I parent, how I coach and how I choose presence over performance. I have two young girls, so the first priority every weekday is ensuring they are ready for school, have had a nutritious breakfast and I enjoy the time I spend with them dropping them off.
2. **Vitality** – The energy and strength I cultivate through movement, nourishment and rest. I intentionally create time in my schedule every day to engage in some sort of physical exercise. If I'm not able to make it to the gym, I'll do a short weights session at home or jump on my Peloton and do a HIIT class.
3. **Fulfilment** – Living in alignment with my purpose and passion. I absolutely love having my own business, coaching leaders, speaking and writing. My schedule is designed with specific allocated hours for work. Occasionally the hours vary based on certain commitments, but they always return to baseline. This also includes learning; I listen to podcasts and audiobooks.
4. **Empowerment** – Honouring my ability to lead, speak up, and create freedom, especially through financial and time autonomy. This includes financial management, personal boundaries and conscious leadership.
5. **Peace** – Nervous system calm, quiet confidence and the boundaries that allow me to live from trust rather than reactivity.

This includes practices like meditation, digital boundaries and time offline.

Values-Led Leadership: Alignment in Action

As a leader, your core values aren't just personal, they're foundational to how you show up for your team, your clients and your business. When you lead from alignment, you lead with clarity, integrity and trust.

Values-led leadership isn't about perfection. It's about consistency between what you believe and how you act. When your decisions reflect your deepest values, others feel it. Your culture strengthens. Your vision becomes magnetic. And your energy stays sustainable because you're not constantly negotiating between who you are and what you're doing.

In a world that's changing rapidly, your values act as your stabiliser. They help you stay grounded, make aligned decisions under pressure and build trust in both you and others.

Balanced Success isn't achieved by accident. It's created when leaders take ownership of their values and let them shape not just their personal life, but their leadership style, communication and strategic decisions.

Leading with values is what keeps your success human and sustainable.

Discovering Your Core Values

Now it's your turn.

Below is a short exercise to help you identify your core values. You'll find a link to a more complete list at the end.

Step 1: Circle What Resonates. Scan through the list of common values below.

Circle every word that speaks to you. Don't overthink things, go with what lands.

Note: This list can also be found online: https://brenebrown.com/resources/dare-to-lead-list-of-values/.

BALANCED SUCCESS

Accountability	Contentment	Fun	Joy	Personal fulfilment	Success
Achievement	Contribution	Future generations	Justice	Power	Teamwork
Adaptability	Cooperation	Generosity	Kindness	Pride	Thrift
Adventure	Courage	Giving back	Knowledge	Recognition	Time
Altruism	Creativity	Grace	Leadership	Reliability	Tradition
Ambition	Curiosity	Gratitude	Learning	Resourcefulness	Travel
Authenticity	Dignity	Growth	Legacy	Respect	Trust
Balance	Diversity	Harmony	Leisure	Responsibility	Truth
Beauty	Efficiency	Health	Love	Risk-taking	Understanding
Being the best	Environment	Home	Loyalty	Safety	Uniqueness
Belonging	Equality	Honesty	Making a difference	Security	Usefulness
Career	Ethics	Hope	Nature	Self-discipline	Vision
Caring	Excellence	Humility	Openness	Self-expression	Vulnerability
Collaboration	Fairness	Humour	Optimism	Self-respect	Wealth
Commitment	Faith	Inclusion	Order	Serenity	Wellbeing
Community	Family	Independence	Parenting	Service	Wholeheartedness
Compassion	Financial stability	Initiative	Patience	Simplicity	Wisdom
Competence	Forgiveness	Integrity	Patriotism	Spirituality	
Confidence	Freedom	Intuition	Peace	Sportsmanship	
Connection	Friendship	Job security	Perseverance	Stewardship	

Step 2: Narrow it Down. From that list, reduce it to your top 10 values. These are the ones that feel like you, even if they're messy or uncomfortable to admit.

Top 10 Values

1. _____
2. _____
3. _____
4. _____
5. _____
6. _____
7. _____
8. _____
9. _____
10. _____

Step 3: Rank Them in Order of Importance. This is where the magic happens. Number your top 10 in order of importance, with one being least important and 10 being most important. This becomes your values hierarchy, a practical tool for understanding how you make decisions and what might be out of alignment in your life right now. To simplify and go deeper, you can also choose to focus on your top 3 - 5.

 Reflection Prompt:

- *Where in my life am I honouring these values?*
- *Where am I in conflict with them?*
- *What small change could I make to live more in alignment this week?*

Your values don't limit you; they liberate you. They offer clarity when things feel confusing. They serve as your compass when you're lost. They guide you back when you've strayed too far.

And when your daily life is aligned with your deepest values? That's where *Balanced Success* begins.

 Key Messages: Mental Wealth: Core Values

- Choose 3–5 values that matter most.
- Write each one as an action.
- Let behaviour prove it.
- Use your values to make decisions.
- Put them in your calendar and budget.
- Decide which value wins if they clash.
- Hold the line under pressure.
- Watch for signs of misalignment.
- Lead by example; your team follows.

How to Complete This Check-In

1. **Rate each area (1–10).**
   1 = off-track/struggling, 5 = mixed/variable, 10 = thriving/consistent.

2. **Add quick notes.**
   In "Notes or Reflections", capture wins, friction points, patterns, triggers, or context (e.g., travel, deadlines).
3. **Choose one tiny upgrade.**
   Pick **one** specific, low-effort change for the next seven days. Aim to "make the good choice the easy choice".

🏛 Balanced Success Check In: Core Values

Area	Score (1-10)	Notes/Reflections
Value Clarity (clear, verb-based)		
Behaviour Alignment (actions match words)		
Boundaries & Trade-Offs (saying no when needed)		
Calendar/Budget Alignment (time & money reflect values)		
Integrity Under Pressure (hold the line when stressed)		

 Reflection Prompt: What's one small boundary I'll set this week to protect a top value?

Mental Wealth: Self Awareness

Know thyself is one of the most important, and challenging, parts of the journey we're all on. As human beings, we are complex and ever-evolving. From the moment we're born, we begin absorbing information from the world around us. Our environment, culture, relationships and energy all shape who we become. Much of how we think, feel and behave as adults reflects our earlier experiences, even the ones we have forgotten.

For leaders, self-awareness isn't a luxury; it's the foundation of trust, influence and impact. Without it, we lead from default patterns, not conscious choice.

Almost all of us have faced struggles, setbacks and pain in life. The way we internalise and respond to those moments becomes part of our wiring. For some, it is a conscious process, driven by a desire to grow or heal. For others, it's unconscious, shaped by survival, conditioning or automatic patterns that no longer serve them.

Self-awareness is a deep and layered topic, with an entire world of research, tools and teachings behind it. But this section isn't here to overwhelm you. It's here to spotlight why this work matters, especially now. If you create the space to explore it, the trajectory of your life can shift in ways you never imagined.

It's time to dig beneath the surface and uncover who you are at your core. Why you think the way you do. Why you repeat certain patterns. And what needs to shift to become the leader and the person you know you're capable of being.

Because when you truly know yourself, everything changes. People sense it. Teams respond to it. And from that place, your leadership becomes more than performance. It becomes power that transforms lives, businesses and the world around you.

Understanding yourself isn't something that happens overnight; it takes consistent focus, time and a willingness to go deep.

After I moved back to Australia, I felt free…but I also felt lost. Everything in my life had changed and for the first time in a long time, I realised I didn't know who I really was or what made me happy. I had spent years living in someone else's shadow, and deep down, I knew it was time to reclaim myself.

So, I began the work that I mentioned in an earlier chapter. Slowly, layer by layer, I peeled back the parts of me that had been shaped by other people's expectations, roles I no longer needed to play, and pain I had buried. Eventually, I arrived at my core; my heart.

I discovered what truly lights me up. I understood why I am the way I am. And for the first time, I could see how my uniqueness was not something to hide, but something that could help others.

Along the way, I let go of ways of thinking and behaving that no longer served me. I released emotions I hadn't realised I was still carrying. And with every release, I became lighter, happier and more *me* than ever before.

Self-Awareness Journey Tools

Building self-awareness is an ongoing journey, and there are a range of tools and practices that can help. Here are some powerful ways to deepen your understanding of yourself:

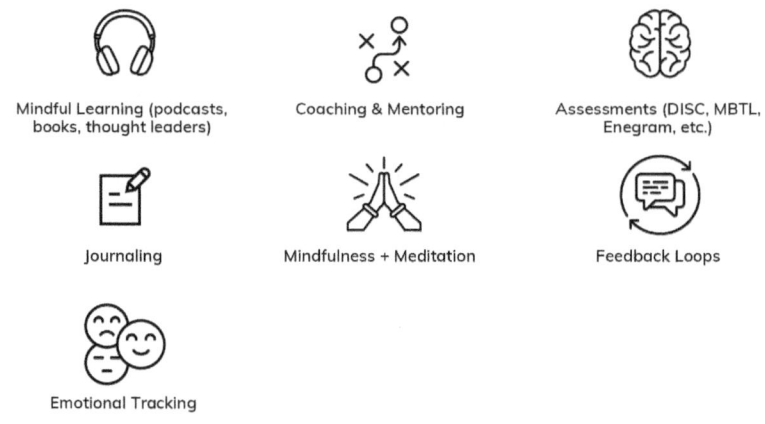

Self-Awareness Toolkit

Consume Mindful Content

Listen to podcasts, watch webinars or YouTube interviews, and read books across topics like emotional intelligence, mindset, leadership, neuroscience and psychology. Some recommended resources include *The School of Life* resources, *Unlocking Us* podcast by Brené Brown, The *Diary of a CEO* podcast, and books like *Emotional Agility* by Susan David or *The Untethered Soul* by Michael A. Singer.

Work with a Coach or Mentor

Partnering with a coach or mentor can accelerate self-awareness. They can hold up a mirror to your thoughts, habits and behaviours in a safe, supportive environment.

Complete Behavioural Assessments

Tools like DISC, MBTI, Enneagram, CliftonStrengths or VIA Character Strengths can reveal patterns in how you think, communicate and operate. While no test defines you completely, they offer a structured way to reflect on your tendencies.

Explore Guided Online Courses

Platforms like Mindvalley, Coursera, InsightTimer, and even MasterClass offer self-development programs that support introspection, emotional mastery or mindfulness.

Journal Regularly

Try prompts like *What did I feel today and why?* or *What patterns keep showing up in my life?* Free writing often uncovers what's beneath the surface.

Practice Mindfulness or Meditation

Even five to 10 minutes a day using apps like Headspace, Calm or Insight Timer can build your self-observing capacity.

Seek Honest Feedback

Ask trusted colleagues, friends or family for feedback on how they experience you. Frame it in a growth-oriented way like, *What's one thing I could improve or be more aware of in how I show up?*

Track Your Emotional States

Use a mood tracker app or simple daily check-in (e.g. rating your mood from 1–10 and noting key triggers).

 Reflection Prompt: Reclaiming Your Core

Now it's your turn to check in with yourself.

Take a moment and ask:
- Where in my life have I been living in someone else's shadow?
- What parts of me have I lost or buried along the way?
- If I were to peel back the layers, what might I find at my core?
- What do I already know lights me up, and what have I been afraid to admit?
- Journal a few thoughts. There's no right or wrong; it's just a starting point.

Boundaries: A Leadership Act of Self-Respect

An important part of self-awareness is protecting your energy. The people in your life play a profound role in your ability to thrive. Supportive, kind and respectful relationships are essential on the journey to *Balanced Success*.

Equally, the presence of toxic or draining individuals, whether subtle or obvious, can take a serious toll on your mental and emotional well-being. One negative interaction can ruin a day, a week or even longer. When those dynamics become embedded, the impact compounds over time.

Here's the truth: you get to choose who has access to you and how t hey treat you.

That doesn't mean it's always easy. Challenging personalities often show up in workplaces, families, social circles and communities. But standing up for yourself, even when it's uncomfortable, signals to the world (and to yourself) that your well-being matters.

Honouring your boundaries is an act of self-respect. It requires courage, honesty and intentional action.

Insights from Brené Brown

In her talk, "Stop Being Too Friendly," researcher and storyteller Brené Brown emphasises that overextending ourselves to please others can lead to resentment and burnout.

Key takeaways:
- Kindness without boundaries leads to resentment.
- You teach people how to treat you.
- Your presence is a privilege, not a right.
- Choose discomfort over resentment.

Practical Steps to Establish Healthy Boundaries

- Limit or cease communication with those who consistently drain you.
- Seek third-party support to establish clear boundaries.
- Document agreements when possible.
- In the workplace, involve HR or supervisors if needed.
- Gradually reduce commitments that no longer serve your growth.

Even small changes can have a significant impact. Boundaries are not barriers, they are bridges to a healthier, more aligned version of you.

Key Messages: Mental Wealth: Self Awareness

- Self-awareness is the foundation of conscious leadership and personal growth.
- It helps you understand your patterns, break free from conditioning and lead from authenticity.
- You can't change what you can't see; awareness is the first step to transformation.
- Healthy boundaries are not walls; they are bridges to a life and leadership style rooted in peace and purpose.

Balanced Success Check-In: Self-Awareness

How to Complete This Check-In

1. **Rate each area (1–10).**
   1 = off-track/struggling, 5 = mixed/variable, 10 = thriving/consistent.
2. **Add quick notes.**
   In "Notes or Reflections", capture wins, friction points, patterns, triggers, or context (e.g., travel, deadlines).

3. **Choose one tiny upgrade.**
   Pick **one** specific, low-effort change for the next seven days. Aim to "make the good choice the easy choice".

- Present-moment awareness today:
- Facts vs story separated:
- Values alignment in choices:
- Supportive self-talk:

Tiny action (choose one):

- Pause and name what I feel.
- Write facts vs story for one situation.
- Do a 2-minute body scan.
- Ask one trusted person for feedback.
- Journal three lines on what mattered today.

Reflection Prompt: *What's one simple cue I'll use this week to pause, check in, and choose my response?*

Mental Wealth: Habits

In the pursuit of *Balanced Success*, habits aren't just helpful, they're foundational.

They form the invisible architecture of your life. What you do repeatedly shapes who you become. For me, *Atomic Habits* (Clear, 2018) was a game changer. After reading it (more than once!), I truly grasped this: our habits today are shaping the future we're walking into.

The small, often unconscious actions we take each day deserve far more attention than we give them. Because those little things? They hold the key.

If *Balanced Success* is the destination, habits are the silent engine that determines whether you'll arrive, and in what state.

BALANCED SUCCESS

On average, habits account for 40–50% of our daily actions, and most are performed unconsciously. Our brains are biologically wired for efficiency, and when an action is repeated often enough, the brain moves it from the conscious to the automatic. At this point, you don't decide to do it, it just happens. This is how you can get up, check your phone, brush your teeth, make your coffee and plan your work day all before you've even consciously "arrived" in the morning. Your conscious mind may be thinking about the meeting ahead, but your body is moving through a script it knows by heart.

This automation is driven by the brain's habit system, which relies heavily on a region called the basal ganglia. Through repetition, strong neural connections are formed and behaviours become "chunked", a kind of internal shortcut that saves precious mental energy. The conscious part of your brain, the prefrontal cortex, is responsible for complex, high-level thinking, but it only represents about 10% of your brain's operations. That means the rest of your actions are managed by unconscious systems.

As a leader navigating a demanding and fast-paced world, protecting and optimising that 10% is critical. You need as much of your cognitive capacity available as possible to inspire, adapt, create change and lead others, especially in a world evolving at unprecedented speed.

So why do habits matter so much?

Because we become what we repeatedly do. If you were to list all your habits today, the helpful, the harmful and the neutral—and project their compounding effect over 20 years, you'd see a version of your future. That projection is built on what you're doing now.

The small choices, the autopilot behaviours, the routines you barely notice...they are either steering you toward the life you want or quietly pulling you off course.

And yet, most people struggle to change their habits. Why?

Because they don't think about them, habits happen beneath awareness. And when people do try to intervene, they often fail because they don't understand how habits actually work. Their conscious effort is no match for an automatic system that's been programmed to conserve energy and resist change.

But here's the good news: habits are changeable. Once you understand the cue-routine-reward loop and how the brain forms habits, you gain the ability to interrupt, redesign and rebuild them. You can create new pathways. You can teach your brain to crave healthier rewards. You can become more intentional in what you repeat, and in doing so, reshape who you become.

The Psychology and Neuroscience Behind Habit Formation

Habits are formed through a loop of cue -> craving -> routine -> reward. When a cue triggers your brain to anticipate a reward, dopamine is released; not when you receive the reward, but in anticipation of it. This creates the craving that drives the behaviour. Over time, as the loop is repeated, strong neural pathways are built and the behaviour becomes automatic, shifting from conscious effort to subconscious execution.

For leaders, this is critical to understand: your brain is constantly seeking efficiency, which means it will favour familiar habits over intentional ones, even if those habits no longer serve you.

The power of habit lies in this: your brain is always learning what to repeat, and dopamine is the mechanism reinforcing the cycle, for better or worse. Becoming aware of these loops gives you the power to interrupt, redesign and rebuild the habits that align with the person you want to be.

Think about it: at a certain point in your day or week, there's usually a cue—for example, it's the end of the day. That cue often triggers a craving, for a sense of reward, comfort or escape. Then comes the routine.

BALANCED SUCCESS

It might be a couple of glasses of red wine, a slice of cake or some doom scrolling on your phone. Finally, you experience the reward, in the form of momentary satisfaction, distraction or relaxation.

This is how habits work; quietly, automatically and often without your permission.

 Reflection Prompt

Take a moment now to identify and write down any negative habits you've formed. What time of day do they tend to occur? What's the cue, the craving and the routine?

This awareness will be helpful as we now explore what those habits are really doing over time.

The Long-Term Impact of Small Actions

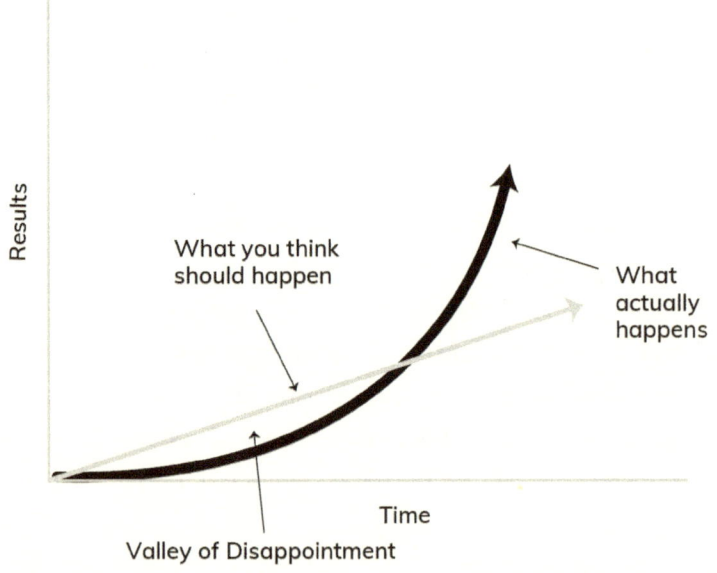

This graph illustrates a frustrating but universal truth about change: results don't appear immediately.

In the beginning, you're showing up, doing the work, staying consistent...but it feels like nothing's happening. This is the Plateau of Latent Potential. You're putting in the effort, but you're not seeing the payoff. Yet.

This is where most people give up.

Think about New Year's resolutions. How many get abandoned by February? Not because people aren't trying, but because they don't see the progress fast enough.

But the truth is, progress is still happening; it's just happening beneath the surface. And often, you're closer than you think. The Valley of Disappointment is that dangerous place just before the curve takes off.

This is the moment to double down. To keep showing up. To trust that change is compounding, even when you can't see it yet.

The breakthrough often comes just after most people quit.

So if you're building something meaningful—whether it's your health, your mindset, your business, or your leadership capacity—this graph is your reminder: **don't stop now**. You might be closer than you think.

Look back at the negative habits you identified earlier. Now ask yourself:
- *If I continue this habit for the next one, five, or 10 years, where is it likely to lead me?*
- *What will be the compounded cost, to my energy, health, mindset, or relationships?*
- *Now imagine replacing that habit with a small, empowering alternative. What might that new trajectory look like?*

Draw your own version of the graph if it helps, with one line for your current habit and another for the habit you want to build.

Sometimes, visualising your future makes the need for change feel more real, and more urgent.

How to Shift Negative Patterns and Strengthen Empowering Ones

Changing a habit isn't about willpower; it's about awareness, strategy and repetition. Most negative patterns are built unconsciously, triggered by cues in your environment or emotional state. To shift them, you first need to identify the cue, routine and reward that drives the loop. Once you've mapped it, you can interrupt the routine and consciously replace it with a more empowering action that delivers a similar reward.

For example, if stress triggers mindless scrolling (routine) to escape discomfort (reward), you might replace it with a walk, deep breathing, or a quick journaling moment, something that soothes your nervous system and builds resilience rather than drains energy.

The key is to:

Make new habits obvious, attractive, easy and satisfying (as James Clear outlines in his "Four Laws of Behaviour Change").

Stack new habits onto existing ones (habit stacking).

Design your environment to support success (reduce friction for good habits and increase it for unhelpful ones).

Repetition is what builds new pathways in the brain, so don't wait for motivation. Focus on small wins, practiced consistently. Every time you repeat an empowering habit, you reinforce the identity of the person you're becoming.

Practical Tools: Habit Stacking, Identity-Based Habits, and Keystone Routines

Transforming your habits isn't about discipline; it's about using the right tools to make change easier and more sustainable. Three of the most effective strategies are:

Habit Stacking

This involves linking a new habit to something you already do. For example, *After I make my morning coffee, I'll write three things I'm grateful for.* Stacking habits onto existing routines reduces decision fatigue and increases follow-through, because the cue is already built into your day.

Identity-Based Habits

Real change happens when you shift from doing to being. Instead of saying, *I want to meditate,* you start saying, *I'm someone who prioritises calm and clarity.* Every habit becomes a vote for the kind of person you want to be. This creates long-term alignment between your actions and your values, which is particularly powerful for leaders who want to lead by example.

Keystone Routines

These are habits that have a ripple effect across multiple areas of life. For example, regular exercise often leads to improved sleep, better food choices and stronger focus at work, all without trying to change those other areas directly. Keystone routines build momentum and make other positive changes easier to sustain.

The most successful habit changes are the ones designed intentionally, starting small and aligned with your identity.

When you systemise your habits instead of relying on motivation, change becomes natural and lasting.

Build Systems That Align With the Leader — and Human — You Want to Be

Goals give you direction, but systems determine your trajectory. Systems are the structures, routines and environments you build around yourself to support the outcomes you want, not just in business, but in life.

To become the kind of leader and human you aspire to be, you must reverse-engineer the habits that person would live by. Ask:
- *If I already were that version of myself, what would my day look like?*
- *What would I consistently do?*
- *What would I no longer tolerate?*

Building aligned systems means:

- Designing your environment to support your highest values.
- Protecting your calendar and energy, so you're not constantly in reaction mode.
- Automating what drains you, and doubling down on what energises and uplifts you.
- Ensuring your daily actions reflect your long-term intentions.

Systems create consistency. And consistency creates identity.

When your systems support who you truly want to become, success becomes inevitable and sustainable.

 Key Messages: Mental Wealth: Habits

- Habits shape nearly half of our daily lives and are often invisible drivers of success or struggle.
- Understanding the neuroscience behind habits (cue-craving-routine-reward) helps you redesign them intentionally.
- Small daily actions compound over time: positive habits accelerate growth, while negative ones quietly erode it.
- Tools like habit stacking, identity-based habits and keystone

routines simplify behaviour change and build lasting results.
- Systems that reflect your long-term goals create the consistency that leads to a sustainable version of *Balanced Success*.

Balanced Success Check-In: Habits

How to Complete This Check-In

1. **Rate each area (1–10).**
   1 = off-track/struggling, 5 = mixed/variable, 10 = thriving/consistent.
2. **Add quick notes.**
   In "Notes or Reflections", capture wins, friction points, patterns, triggers, or context (e.g., travel, deadlines).

- **Choose one tiny upgrade.**
  Pick **one** specific, low-effort change for the next seven days. Aim to "make the good choice the easy choice". Awareness of negative habits Consistency this week: __
- Clarity of next action: __
- Environment supports the habit: __
- Friction removed: __

Tiny action (choose one):

- Write tomorrow's single next step.
- Set a cue or reminder.
- Prep the environment now.
- Remove one friction or trigger.
- Track today's habit in two linesNow ask yourself:
  - *What is one tiny shift I can make this week that reflects the kind of leader, and human, I want to become?*

Write your commitment below and revisit it daily.

Because over time, those small steps shape everything.

Mental Wealth: Resilience

> *"Do not judge me by my successes, judge me by how many times I fell down and got back up again."*
> **- Nelson Mandela.**

We all experience challenges, struggles and pain in our lives in varying degrees. Many people choose to fall victim to their circumstances, which often projects as blame, avoidance and failing to grow. Others can wade through murky waters and, inch by inch, step by step, somehow make it to the shoreline. They arrive at the "other side" of the struggle which not only provides them with a sense of relief, but in the process they have emerged as a different person; a stronger one, a wiser one, a more resilient one.

In the coming years, almost every system we rely on—education, employment, leadership, healthcare, even identity—will be tested or transformed. The ripple effect of this change will be deeply personal. For many, it will manifest as increased levels of stress, fear, confusion and emotional exhaustion.

For many leaders, this will be a particularly testing time. You won't just be responsible for strategies and outcomes. You'll be the emotional compass for your team. You'll need to regulate your own state while holding space for others. You'll need to face challenges with grounded optimism, flexible thinking and inner strength, not blind positivity, but embodied resilience.

True resilience is not glamorous. It's uncomfortable. It forces you to stare your fears in the face, confront your weaknesses and still whisper, *I won't quit today. No matter what.*

Stress: The Silent Thief of Resilience

Resilience is fundamentally about your capacity to recover from or adapt to stress, whether that's physical, emotional or mental. It's not about avoiding stress altogether (which is impossible for leaders), but about how effectively you recognise, respond to and recover from it.

Let's be honest—most leaders don't realise how stressed they are until their body forces them to stop. It's not the big, dramatic events that usually get us. It's the slow drip, the micro stress doses, that accumulate day after day until we find ourselves overwhelmed, exhausted, or emotionally frayed…and we can't quite pinpoint why.

Stress has shown up for me in the past in ways I never expected. It wasn't the textbook symptoms I was told to watch for. For me, it looked like sharp, random stabs in my stomach, which I brushed off as having eaten something bad. My hair started falling out in clumps, but I blamed a new hair product. I forgot a close friend's birthday completely, something I would never normally do, but I chalked it up to being "just busy", I wasn't connecting the dots…not yet.

I've come to understand that stress isn't just about being "busy" or "under pressure". It's about being disconnected from the pace your body and mind were actually designed to operate at. It's about ignoring the whispers such as the foggy brain, the low energy or the short fuse, until they become screams.

Physician and author Dr Rangan Chatterjee, in *The Stress Solution* (2019), refers to stress as the hidden epidemic of the 21st century. And he's right. For many of us, stress has become so normal that we don't even question it anymore. But just because something is common, it doesn't mean it's healthy.

In fact, most of the stress we carry isn't caused by major life events; it's built up through hundreds of micro stressors every day: the unread emails, the constant pings from your phone, the tension in a relationship, the mental load of decision-making, the pressure to keep up. Dr Chatterjee calls these Micro Stress Doses (MSDs), and they're silently eroding our energy and resilience, without us even realising it.

Think about a typical day: You wake up to an alarm, already feeling behind in your day, scroll your phone while brushing your teeth and start mentally prepping for the day before you've even made a cup of tea. Then comes the pressure of getting kids ready or rushing to beat the traffic, followed by a barrage of meetings, problems to solve and decisions to make, often without space to pause. Somewhere in there you might grab something to eat, probably while answering emails. A tense conversation with a colleague, an unresolved issue at home or the endless stream of notifications only adds to the internal clutter. By the time the day ends, you've had no real break, and your body is still running on adrenaline…but you tell yourself you're "fine".

This is how MSDs add up. Not with one big blowout, but with a thousand tiny leaks in the system. And when left unchecked, they chip away at your energy, patience, health and clarity, making it harder to lead with strength and purpose.

Why This Matters for Leaders

Management of stress matters because stress doesn't just affect your mood; it affects your ability to lead, to think clearly, to sleep well, to regulate your emotions and to show up for the people who matter. It compromises your health, your patience, your creativity and your clarity.

And here's the truth: You cannot build true resilience if stress is running your life from the shadows.

This section isn't about eliminating stress altogether; that's unrealistic. Instead, it's about learning to recognise it sooner, reduce its impact and build the tools to navigate it with more strength, presence and clarity. Because resilience doesn't mean pushing through at all costs; it means knowing how to bounce back with wisdom and awareness.

10 Stress Reset Strategies for Leaders

Stress will always be part of leadership, but burnout doesn't have to be. Here are practical ways to regulate your nervous system, protect your energy and lead from a place of grounded clarity:

1. Start your day before the world does.
2. Name what's really draining you.
3. Break the mental loop with movement.
4. Breathe like it matters, because it does.
5. Protect your white space.
6. Digitally disconnect, on purpose.
7. Practice micro recoveries.
8. Get sunlight and fresh air daily.
9. Talk it out, don't tough it out.
10. Redefine success as sustainability.

What Makes Up Resilience?

Resilience isn't just one thing; it's a combination of mental, emotional and behavioural capacities that leaders can develop over time.

Core components include:
- Emotional regulation.
- Mental agility.
- Purpose and meaning.
- Optimism (realistic, not naive).
- Self-awareness.
- Connection.
- Recovery.
- Agency and accountability.

Tanya's Insights – Building My Resilience Muscle

"It ain't about how hard you hit. It's about how hard you can get hit and keep moving forward. That's how winning is done."
— Rocky Balboa

When I was younger, I watched Sylvester Stallone in the movie *Rocky Balboa*, and this quote landed hard. It wasn't about boxing; it was about life. About having the strength to get back up when life knocks you flat. That idea shaped how I see resilience to this day.

Running a business has tested me in ways I could never have imagined. I thought I was doing all the right things—building a solid team, investing in the right spaces, planning for growth—and yet something completely unexpected blindsided me.

After a series of wins and consistent growth, 2012 came along, and I genuinely thought our business was about to go under. Within a single month, our two biggest clients, both major oil and gas companies, decided to take their IT operations in-house. Just like that, 30% of our revenue was about to disappear. I was responsible for the operational side of the business including finance, strategy and really, the works, so I felt responsible for everything.

My initial thought was: *That's it. We're done.* We'd already stretched ourselves financially with a beautiful office space and a high-performing team. There was no room for error. I stopped sleeping. My stress boiled over into arguments with my business partner. And inside, I carried a growing sense of doom; it was like I was backed into a dark alley and there was no way out.

But here's the truth about resilience: you don't get to stay in the alley. You get up. You walk forward towards the light. Even if it's just one step at a time.

That's what I did. Bit by bit, we created a plan, and we executed it swiftly and decisively. Through resilience, we didn't just survive. We strengthened our resolve along with our business, and got through it all without losing a single team member or compromising the integrity of our company.

And from that point forward, I truly understood the saying: *It doesn't get easier. You get stronger.*

The Resilient Leader's Ripple Effect

You might never see all the ways your resilience impacts others. But every time you choose to take a breath instead of react, every time you model calm in a crisis, every time you bounce back and choose growth over blame…

You lead differently.

You give your team permission to be human. You build a culture that values honesty, recovery and progress, not perfection. Resilience isn't a solo act. It's a ripple.

And in a world that's changing fast, your ability to rise wiser, not just stronger, might be the most powerful leadership move you ever make.

Key Messages: Mental Wealth: Resilience

- Resilience is built through adversity, not comfort.
- Micro stress doses (MSDs) are the silent thief of energy and clarity.
- Stress is part of leadership, but burnout doesn't have to be.
- Emotional regulation and mental agility are critical to modern resilience.
- Resilience is a muscle that strengthens through awareness, recovery and action.
- The ripple effect of a resilient leader transforms teams, culture and outcomes.

Balanced Success Check-In: Resilience

How to Complete This Check-In

1. **Rate each area (1–10).**
   1 = off-track/struggling, 5 = mixed/variable, 10 = thriving/consistent.
2. **Add quick notes.**
   In "Notes or Reflections", capture wins, friction points, patterns, triggers, or context (e.g., travel, deadlines).
3. **Choose one tiny upgrade.**
   Pick **one** specific, low-effort change for the next seven days. Aim to "make the good choice the easy choice."

- I recognise the early signs of stress in my body and behaviour: ___
- I prioritise recovery — not just productivity: ___
- I use healthy coping strategies when things get tough: ___
- I model grounded resilience for those around me: ___
- I bounce back from setbacks with perspective and action: ___

> **Reflection Prompt:** *What is one small, consistent practice I can commit to that will build my resilience muscle this month?*

Mental Wealth: Clarity

Clarity is the clean line between noise and what matters, the moment you stop scattering your energy and start choosing the few things that truly move the needle, so your time, attention and decisions align with the life and leadership you are here to build.

My schedule includes dedicated time to think without distraction. What I do in that time varies. Sometimes I lie in my infrared light bed. Other times, I meditate or simply sit and watch the natural world unfold around me. I've had some of my most profound *aha* moments during these quiet pauses. And on other days, it's just about reconnecting with myself after a full, fast-paced week.

I've come to understand the quiet power of these simple acts.

But it wasn't always this way...

In a world specifically designed to confuse, distract and overwhelm, obtaining clarity is becoming increasingly difficult. We jump from one thing to another all day, sometimes consciously, but often unconsciously. Over time, our sense of direction—of what's truly "left" or "right" for us—becomes degraded, and we find ourselves operating in a fog of confusion.

So what is clarity? According to the Merriam-Webster Dictionary, clarity is defined as "the quality of being clear".

Being clear isn't something most people talk about; it's rarely the focus of a business workshop, and it's almost never the topic of conversation at the dinner table. It's the forgotten hero. As Brené Brown stated, "Clear is kind. Unclear is unkind." (Brown, 2018). It's power lies in its simplicity and yet, its impact is profound. It's about being able to think clearly.

I can almost see the puzzled looks. How does one actually do that?

We've become so lost in our oversaturated and overcomplicated lives that we've forgotten the value of making space to clear the noise. Think about it; most of us can't even resist looking at our phones when we're in an elevator or sitting in a waiting room at the doctor's. We fill the space with "stuff" because that has become more comfortable than…well, just doing nothing. Just being.

Being present means inhabiting the moment without intention. It means listening to the sounds around you, observing your environment and letting your thoughts flow without needing to control them. Presence dissolves the mental resistance built up from the chaos of the day. It lets go of the emotions and stories that are no longer serving you. And in doing so, your mind becomes free, to think, to breathe and to just *be*.

Why Clarity Matters for Leaders

Clarity isn't just a nice to have. It's a core leadership asset. Research and business performance data continue to show that clarity improves decision-making, reduces stress and accelerates meaningful action.

Here are five research-backed reasons clarity is essential for leadership success:

1. Clarity drives better decision-making

McKinsey research shows senior leaders spend roughly 37–40% of their time on decision making, and 61% say at least half of that time is used ineffectively. This is why clarity matters: it reduces bias and "noise" so that choices align with values, priorities and long-term outcomes. Clarity also counters cognitive biases and variability ("system noise") that quietly degrade decision quality.

Clarity brings intentionality. Without it, you're simply reacting.

2. Clarity reduces cognitive overload

Neuroscience shows that the brain's prefrontal cortex, responsible for focus, planning and reasoning, performs poorly under constant ambiguity. When clarity is lacking, cognitive fatigue sets in. This leads to mental exhaustion, poor focus and emotional reactivity. Clarity reduces mental noise, which frees up executive function and improves performance.

Harvard Business School researchers found that employees who spent 15 minutes at the end of each day reflecting in writing performed ~23% better on a final assessment than those who didn't; evidence that brief, structured reflection can boost clarity and subsequent performance.

3. Clarity fuels confidence and action

McKinsey research found strategic clarity and role clarity to be core behaviours in healthy, high-performing organisations. When leaders lack clarity, they hesitate. They second-guess. Teams feel the ripple effect. Conversely, clear leaders act with conviction and inspire confidence in others. Clarity is a self-trust amplifier. You don't need to know every step, but you do need to know the direction.

Clarity doesn't mean certainty. It means knowing what matters most right now.

4. Clarity improves communication

Gallup's engagement research highlights clear expectations as a foundational driver of performance and engagement; teams that score high on "I know what is expected of me at work" are more productive. At the same time, only 13% of employees strongly agree their leadership communicates effectively, showing how unclear communication fuels confusion and disengagement. When leaders communicate clearly, people know what to do, why it matters, and how they contribute.

Clear communication starts with a clear mind.

5. Clarity enhances personal wellbeing

A lack of clarity creates anxiety. It is the emotional equivalent of standing in a dark forest without a torch. You keep moving, but you are unsure if it is the right direction. Leaders who gain clarity report feeling calmer, more focused and more present, which improves relationships, health and overall fulfilment (Coutts, Al-Kire and Weidler, 2023). Clarity does not mean certainty. It means knowing what matters most right now.

Simple, Science-Backed Practices for Mental Clarity

Clarity isn't something that appears out of nowhere; it's something we make space for. You don't need a 10-day retreat to find it. Sometimes, it's as simple as going for a walk or a run without your phone, or switching it to *Do Not Disturb* so your mind can catch its breath.

Other times, it's about making a non-negotiable date with nature—sitting under a tree, by the ocean or in your own backyard with no agenda other than to simply be there. And for many people, a daily meditation practice, even just a few minutes, can act as a powerful mental declutter, helping to reset and reconnect with what truly matters.

These practices aren't luxuries. In a noisy world, they are leadership essentials. They help you filter out what's urgent but unimportant, and reconnect to what's true. They return you to yourself.

Here are some accessible, research-supported ways to create clarity:
1. Silent walking.
2. Mindfulness meditation.
3. Nature immersion.
4. Reflective journaling.
5. Breathwork exercises.
6. Digital Detox periods.
7. Early morning walks.
8. Mindful eating.
9. Scheduled 'white space'.

10. Connecting with purpose.

Clarity and the *Balanced Success* **Life**

In a life that's aligned and well-balanced, clarity acts as a compass. It's the space between reactivity and intention; the ability to tune into what really matters, rather than getting lost in noise.

Without clarity, we chase the wrong goals, say yes to the wrong things, and ignore the whispers of our intuition.

Balanced Success isn't about doing more, it's about doing what matters most. And that starts with being clear. Clear on your values. Clear on your energy. Clear on where you're heading and why. Clarity allows you to say *no* with confidence and *yes* with alignment. In the *Balanced Success* model, clarity sits at the heart of self-leadership. Without it, every other area, from health to relationships to purpose, is clouded by confusion or misalignment.

Clarity creates calm. It reduces the noise so you can hear yourself think again. And when you can think clearly, you can lead clearly.

 Key Messages: Mental Wealth: Clarity

- Clarity is the foundation of intentional leadership and personal alignment. It helps reduce cognitive overload, improve communication and foster confident action.
- Simple daily practices, such as meditation, journaling and digital detox, create space for clarity to emerge.
- In the *Balanced Success* life, clarity is your internal compass, guiding choices from a place of truth, not pressure.
- You don't need more time; you need more clarity on what matters most.

Balanced Success Check-In: Clarity

On a scale of 1 to 10, with one being, *I'm scattered, reactive and unsure what really matters*, and 10 being *I'm clear, focused and confidently aligned with what matters most*, how would you rate your current level of clarity in life and leadership?

Take a moment to reflect: *What's one small action you can take this week to create more mental space or intentional clarity?*

Mental wealth is not built in a single decision or moment, it is cultivated through consistent choices that honour your resilience, clarity, habits, self-awareness and values.

It is the unseen currency that fuels every part of life and leadership.

When you invest in it, you create a foundation that steadies you through change, expands your capacity to lead with integrity and allows you to live in alignment with what matters most.

True wealth is not just what sits in your bank account; it is the strength, balance and clarity within you that no one can take away.

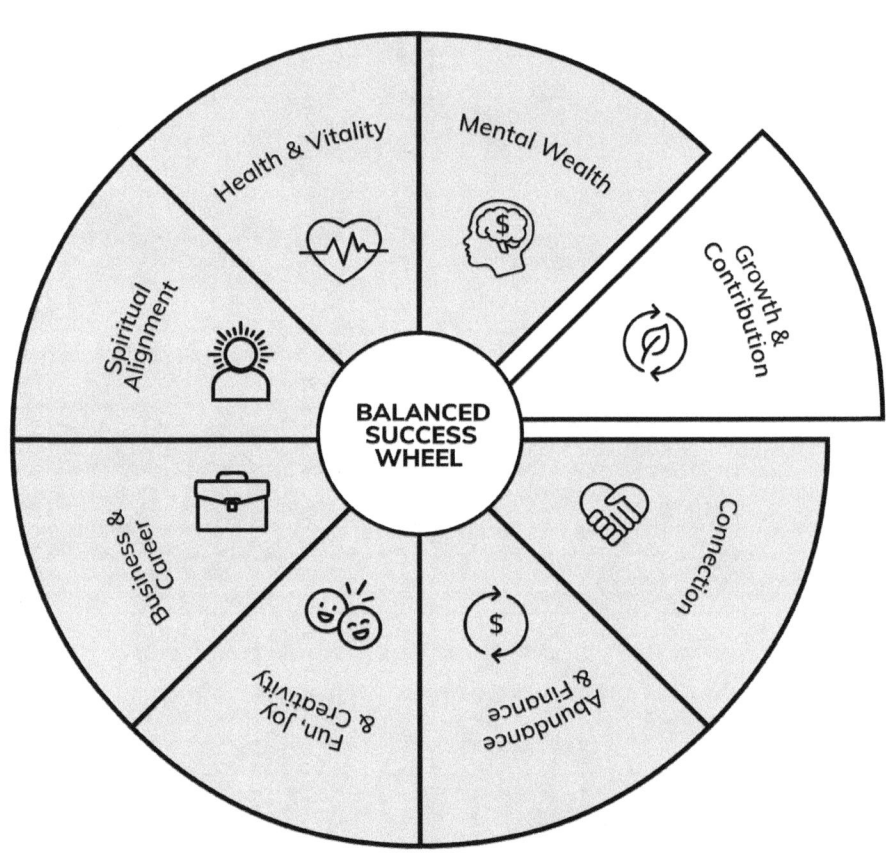

CHAPTER SEVEN

Growth and Contribution

*"Live as if you were to die tomorrow.
Learn as if you were to live forever."*
— Mahatma Gandhi

I'm proud to say I've had a growth mindset for as long as I can remember. Maybe it stems from my days as a competitive runner. Or maybe it's just in my DNA. Either way, one thing is certain; I love learning and I'll never stop.

I find ways to learn almost every day. Whether it's through a podcast, a conversation, a book or a reflective moment; it keeps my brain healthy, my thinking sharp and my perspective current. In a world that's saturated, noisy and constantly changing, growth is what keeps you relevant. And more importantly, it keeps you, *you*.

Having a "student of life" mindset will serve you well in the long game of life.

Your life is constantly evolving—you, the people around you, your organisation and the world at large. As a leader, it's essential that you never stop learning. Growth requires curiosity, humility, and an open mind, especially when it comes to topics outside your natural interests or strengths.

Sticking only to what you're comfortable with or burying your head in the sand on important issues will hold you back, not just in business, but in life. The difference between a good leader and a great one often comes down to one thing: a consistent, intentional approach to learning.

We all have subjects we gravitate toward, whether it's leadership, mindset, politics, health or AI. But great leaders build breadth and depth. They carve out time to grow, even when they're busy. Because the truth is, *not enough time* is an excuse that doesn't cut the mustard anymore. If you're not learning and growing, you're stagnating. And in today's world, stagnation doesn't just slow you down; it leaves you behind.

That said, it's not always easy. The volume of content we're exposed to today can feel overwhelming. From books and podcasts to online courses and trending LinkedIn debates, the pressure to stay "up-to-date" is relentless. And when you're trying to live a balanced life, keeping up with everything is not only unrealistic, it's unsustainable.

Then there's AI. The revolution isn't just approaching, it's already here. The doors haven't been knocked on; they've been kicked down. The pressure for leaders to not only understand tools like large language models, but to embrace them to keep their organisations relevant, is at an all-time high. Avoiding it is no longer an option.

Navigating Information Overload

In today's world, the challenge isn't access to information, it's filtering it. We live in an era in which every podcast, newsletter, headline, audiobook, Substack and 60-second clip is competing for our attention. The problem is: your attention is finite and your energy even more so.

If you're a leader trying to stay current, the pressure can be exhausting. You're expected to know about global trends, industry shifts, innovation, policy changes, people management, mindset frameworks, wellness, parenting, politics…the list goes on.

It's not just that there's too much information. It's that there's too much poorly filtered information. Most people are reacting, scrolling or dabbling in surface-level inputs without any structure or intention. This leads to what I call cognitive bloating—too much input, not enough digestion. You're mentally full, but not actually nourished.

Just like your body thrives on clean, intentional nutrition, your mind needs the same.

Here's the truth: more learning is not always better learning. What matters is strategic, well-integrated learning that serves your leadership, your values and your future.

To cut through the noise, you need to:

Choose quality over volume.

Subscribe to one or two high-value sources per topic, not 10. Follow creators or experts who stretch your thinking, not just echo what you already know.

- **Create a "Growth Window".**
  Set aside consistent time, even just 20 minutes a day, for intentional learning. This could be your commute, a morning ritual or time blocked between meetings.

- **Don't consume passively.**
  Take notes. Highlight insights. Reflect. Ask, *How will I use this? Does this support where I want to grow?* Don't just collect content, integrate it.
- **Create a growth plan.**
  Just like you'd train for a marathon or event, map out your learning like a personal training program. Why treat your intellectual development any differently? Mix your modalities—podcasts, books, courses, conversations—and plan both professional and personal learning in a balanced way.
- **Know when to stop**
  Overconsumption leads to cognitive fatigue. Sometimes growth means pausing and applying what you already know. Less input, more embodiment.
- This is where balanced success really shows up: not in how much you know, but in how wisely you manage what you let in.

Design Your 90-Day Growth Plan

> *"Growth doesn't just happen."*
> — **John C. Maxwell, author and orator**

Just like you wouldn't enter a marathon without a training program, your growth as a leader deserves the same level of thought and intention.

Use the following framework to build a personalised growth plan for the next 90 days; one that supports both your professional development and your personal alignment.

1. **Choose Your Growth Focus Areas.**
   Pick one area from each category:
   - **Skill Development:** e.g. Public speaking, AI literacy, strategic planning, coaching skills.
   - **Mindset Expansion:** e.g. Emotional regulation, resilience, letting

go of control, growth mindset.
- **New Perspective or Topic:** e.g. Environmental sustainability, youth trends, indigenous knowledge, behavioural science.

2. **Select Your Modalities.**

    How will you learn and engage? Choose 2–3 WAYS you enjoy or can stick with:
- Audiobook / podcast series.
- Online training program or seminar.
- Book (paper or Kindle).
- Mastermind or peer group.
- Mentoring or coaching conversations.
- Reflective journaling or note-taking.

3. **Schedule It In.**

    Block out time in your calendar. Make it visual. This is training, not optional scrolling.
- Growth Window: ____ mins per day / ____ times per week.
- Integration Time: ____ mins per week to reflect or apply.
- Review Date: Set a checkpoint in 30 or 60 days to assess your progress.

4. **Your Growth Statement.**

    In the next 90 days, I will grow in the areas of ___, ___, and ___ by engaging in ___, ___, and ___.

Repeat it. See it. Live it.

Contribution – Leading Through Service

For a long time, I had the mindset that contribution was something I'd get around to later in life, when I had more time. And that was before I had kids. Back then, work consumed my energy, and in the little spare time I had, I filled the gaps with socialising at nice bars and restaurants.

Life looked full, but something was missing.

Now, I see contribution differently. I realise how grounding, fulfilling and meaningful it feels to give in small ways, whether that's donating to a cause I care about, helping a local event or showing up for someone who needs support.

You don't have to lead a movement or start a foundation to make an impact. Taking time to contribute—in your home, business, community, or beyond—carries ripple effects far greater than we realise. Even the smallest acts can shift your energy and reconnect you with something bigger than yourself.

Benefits of Everyday Contribution

- A sense of belonging to something beyond yourself and a reminder that you're part of a wider community.
- The chance to build new and diverse connections.
- Role modelling generosity and values-based leadership for your team, family and children.
- The opportunity to develop new skills, interests and confidence through service.

Tanya's Experience: Contribution Begins with Connection

After the birth of my second child and a move to a new neighbourhood, I found myself feeling lost and disconnected. I didn't know many people in the area, and I was craving a sense of community, specifically to be around other business-minded women who were also navigating motherhood.

For years, I had thrown myself into professional networking events, in both Australia and New York City, but by this point, I was burnt out on surface-level conversations and transactional meet-ups. I didn't want to show up in heels and with pitch decks. I wanted something real. Something grounded. Something with heart.

But after some searching, I couldn't find the group I was looking for.

Instead of giving up, I remembered a networking model I'd been part of in the city, one that did things differently. It was more intentional, more human. So, without overthinking it, I reached out to the founders and asked if I could replicate the concept in my area, this time with a clear focus: women in business who were also mums.

Within weeks, the group took off. We had 25 women showing up regularly.

What started as a simple idea quickly grew into something meaningful, not just for me, but for everyone involved. It became more than a networking group. It became a safe space. A circle of support. A place where friendships were formed, collaborations emerged and people felt truly seen.

That experience reminded me of something powerful: contribution doesn't have to be complicated. Sometimes, it's simply about creating what you wish existed .and inviting others in.

Contribution in Action: Simple Ways to Give Back

- Volunteer at a local community or school event.
- Donate to a cause aligned with your values.
- Offer mentorship to someone earlier in their journey.
- Start or join a community group with purpose.
- Give your time or skills to a not-for-profit or local business.
- Organise a clean-up day, fundraiser, or care package initiative.
- Support a friend or colleague who's struggling, with presence, not just advice.
- Model contribution in your family—involve your kids in giving and service.

Final Words: Contribution Is a Two-Way Gift

Contribution isn't just about what you give, it's about what you gain. A deeper sense of meaning. Stronger relationships. A grounded perspective. When you contribute, you reconnect with what really matters and remember that your life, your energy and your leadership exist within a much bigger ecosystem.

Don't wait for the perfect time. Don't overcomplicate it. Start small. Start now. The ripple effect might surprise you.

 Key Messages:

- Growth is a conscious, ongoing process, not something that happens by accident.
- Leaders thrive when they embrace a "student of life" mindset, even amidst complexity and change.
- Strategic learning and curated inputs matter more than volume.
- Contribution offers a deep sense of fulfilment, belonging and grounded service.
- Both growth and giving reconnect us with our purpose and elevate our leadership.

Balanced Success Check-In – Growth & Contribution

Instructions
1. **Rate each line (1–10)** in the blank.
2. 1–3 = off-track, 4–6 = building, 7–8 = consistent, 9–10 = integrated.
3. **Add one quick note** beside any line (e.g., an example, friction point, or win).
4. **Choose one small action** for the lowest-scoring line for the next seven days.

- I have a growth mindset and regularly engage in learning that challenges me.
- I curate what I consume to support my values and leadership direction.
- I make time for meaningful contribution, even in small ways.
- I feel connected to something bigger than myself.

Reflection Prompt: *What's one area of growth and one small act of contribution you can commit to in the next seven days?*

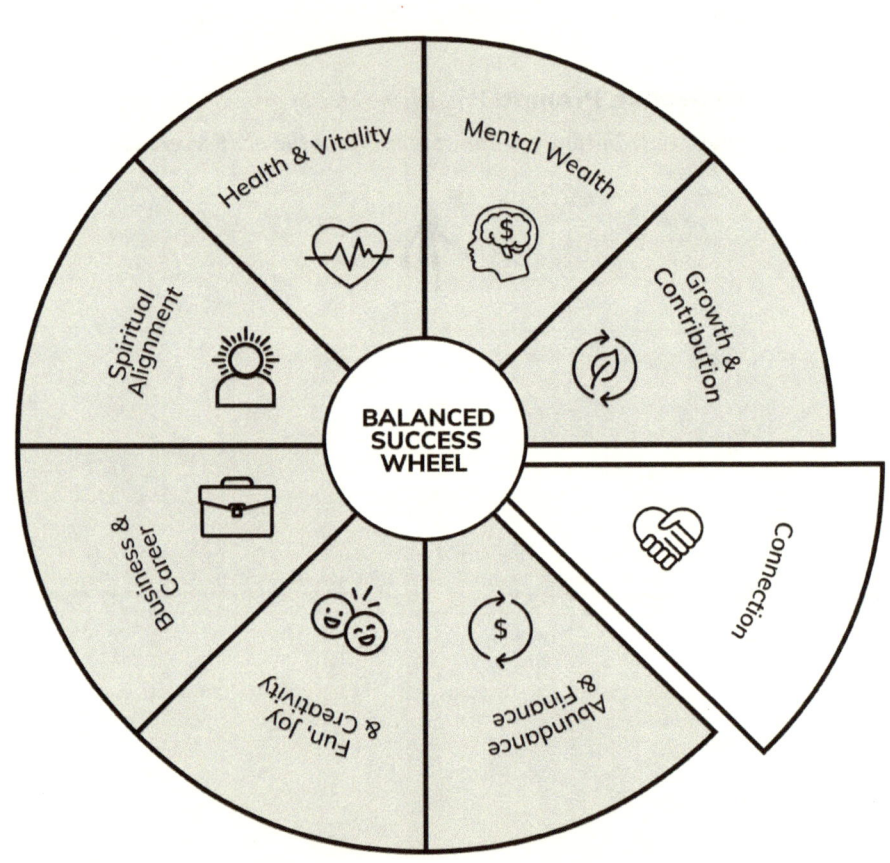

CHAPTER EIGHT
Connection

"Connection is why we're here. It is what gives purpose and meaning to our lives."
— **Brené Brown**

As humans, we are wired for connection. Meaningful relationships aren't just nice to have, they're vital to our health and wellbeing. When we connect with others, especially in acts of kindness or shared purpose, our brain releases oxytocin, often called the "bonding hormone". It's responsible for that warm, connected feeling, and research shows it plays a significant role in reducing stress, improving emotional resilience and even supporting long-term cardiovascular health.

In a world that often celebrates independence, high achievement and digital efficiency, we can easily forget the essential human truth: we are wired for connection. And not just surface-level interaction, but real, soul-deep connection that grounds us, mirrors our truth and reminds us we're not alone in the journey.

For many high performers, connection gets sacrificed at the altar of busy.

We build businesses, lead teams and manage households, but often neglect our need for emotional intimacy and meaningful relationships. The irony is this: the more successful we become, the more isolated we tend to feel, unless we actively protect and prioritise connection.

Tanya's Story:
From Disconnection to the Gift of Being Seen

When I'm under intense pressure at work, everything else starts to fade. Balance slips quietly out the back door while I hyper-focus on only one or two areas of my *Balanced Success Wheel*. At first, it feels manageable. I convince myself it's temporary. But eventually, like clockwork, the cracks begin to show.

At times when I have edged closer to the precipice of complete misalignment in my life, one of the first things I have let go of has been connection. At these times, I stopped replying to messages. I withdrew from invitations. I became unavailable to the people who mattered most—my friends and family. And while that might sound like a common pattern, it became particularly dangerous when I was living overseas.

When I was at my lowest point in New York City, when my personal and professional lives felt like they were imploding, every minute of every day, my closest friends and family were back home in Australia. They didn't know what was happening and I didn't let them. Hiding felt safer than reaching out and admitting how far I had fallen. How out of balance my life had become. I was deeply lonely, but still wearing the mask of someone who had it all together.

What saved me was a small handful of beautiful friends I met while living in NYC. They saw me, really saw me. They cared. They listened. They offered me their time, their kindness, their quiet companionship. That contribution, and that connection, at a time when I felt emotionally invisible, was a lifeline. Without them, I don't know what I would have done.

Their presence reminded me: connection heals. It doesn't need to be big or loud. It just needs to be real.

Why Connection Matters

Connection is not a "nice to have". It's a biological and psychological need.

Harvard's 85-year Study of Adult Development (1938-present) found that the single most important predictor of long-term health and happiness wasn't wealth, fame, or success, it was the quality of our relationships. People who were more socially connected to family, friends and community lived longer, were happier and experienced slower mental decline

Have you ever stopped and considered what you think about when you are resting? For many of us, it's about reverting to thinking about people and relationships. Social connection is as essential to our survival as food and water.

BALANCED SUCCESS

A 2023 meta-analysis published in *Nature Human Behaviour* confirms that chronic loneliness increases the risk of early death by up to 45%, linking social disconnection with heart disease, cognitive decline and mental health deterioration.

In the context of *Balanced Success,* connection isn't just about people, it's about:
- Being seen and understood without judgment.
- Having people in your life who call you forward and hold you accountable.
- Creating micro-moments of joy and presence in your everyday interactions.
- Feeling safe enough to share your truth and receive feedback.

Connection Starts With You

Before we can connect with others, we must reconnect with ourselves. That means getting quiet enough to ask:
- *What do I really need right now?*
- *Where am I feeling disconnected, from my truth, my body, my values?*
- *Have I become emotionally unavailable to myself?*

Self-connection is the foundation of external connection. When we numb, perform, or stay constantly busy, we abandon ourselves, and others can feel that.

> *"Loneliness and the feeling of being unwanted is the most terrible poverty."*
> — **Mother Teresa.**

Building Meaningful Relationships

Real connection isn't built in the boardroom or over a performance review. It's created in the quiet moments: when we're present with our kids, when we look someone in the eye without a phone in hand, when we say *me too* instead of pretending we have it all together.

To nurture true connection:
- Put the phone down. Presence is the new luxury.
- Say what you really mean. Vulnerability creates emotional intimacy.
- Schedule relationships, not just results. Make time for connection like you do for meetings.
- Join or create communities. Circles of aligned people (such as women's groups, masterminds, etc.) are the antidote to professional loneliness.

The Cost of Disconnection

When we disconnect for too long, we pay the price. It shows up as irritability, burnout, resentment, overconsumption and a deep feeling of emptiness that no amount of external success can fill. You may feel it as:
- *I'm surrounded by people, but I feel alone.*
- *I don't have anyone I can really talk to.*
- *I don't feel seen or valued for who I truly am.*

According to Dr. Julianne Holt-Lunstad, a leading researcher on social connection, social isolation has a greater risk factor for mortality than obesity or physical inactivity. In the leadership world, this disconnection leads to decision fatigue, empathy erosion and eventually, a dangerous kind of numbness. These are red flags and invitations to realign.

Balanced Success Tool: The Connection Audit

Draw three circles:
1. Inner Circle – Deep emotional connections (3–5 people max).
2. Middle Circle – Trusted friends, colleagues, or mentors.
3. Outer Circle – Acquaintances, professional networks, community groups.

Now ask yourself:

- *Who is missing from your inner circle?*
- *Who do you want to reconnect with?*
- *What relationships no longer feel aligned?*

Take a moment to reflect:
- *Who in your life truly sees you?*
- *Who do you feel most yourself around?*
- *Who have you lost touch with that you miss?*
- *When was the last time you really connected—with someone, or with yourself?*

Connection is your anchor. It's what keeps you human, heart-led and whole. In the age of AI and accelerating change, leaders who stay connected—to their people, their purpose, and their inner world—will not only survive, they will lead us forward.

Key Messages: Connection

- Connection starts with self.
- Presence beats performance.
- Depth over breadth.
- Listen to understand, not to reply.
- Consistency builds trust.
- Vulnerability invites closeness.
- Boundaries protect genuine connection.
- Repair ruptures quickly.
- Curate your spaces (people, places, platforms).
- Small, intentional moments matter most.

Balanced Success Check-In — Connection

Instructions

How to Complete This Check-In

1. **Rate each area (1–10).**
   1 = off-track/struggling, 5 = mixed/variable, 10 = thriving/consistent.

2. **Add quick notes.**
   In "Notes or Reflections", capture wins, friction points, patterns, triggers, or context (e.g., travel, deadlines).

3. **Choose one tiny upgrade.**
   Pick **one** specific, low-effort change for the next seven days. Aim to "make the good choice the easy choice."

- Connection to self:
- Connection to others:
- Presence (distraction -> focus):

 **Tiny action (choose one):**

- Send one sincere thank-you.
- Make a 10-minute no-agenda call.
- Share a quiet, phone-free moment with someone.
- Commit (one line):

👥 **Reflection Prompt:**

Today I felt most connected when:

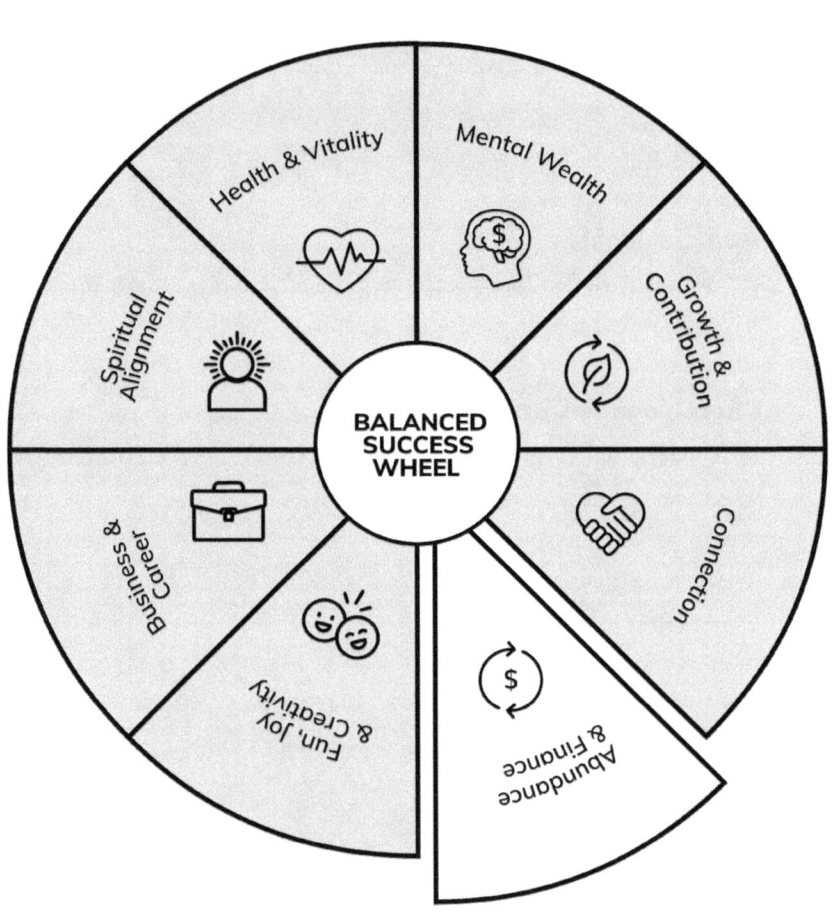

CHAPTER NINE

Abundance & Finance

In the introduction, we named two truths: success without fulfillment is hollow, and the age of AI demands grounded, resourced leaders. Both require energy you can count on. Money is one form of that energy—neutral until we give it meaning—and it either fuels your mission or quietly drains it.

In the *Balanced Success* model, finance isn't separate from wellbeing; it funds it. The choices you make with money ripple into your health, relationships, leadership and long-term impact. When money is chaotic, clarity, confidence and capacity shrink. When money is aligned, everything else gets breathing room.

This chapter is a reset. Not spreadsheets and shame; alignment and agency. We'll look at your story with money, the emotions underneath it and the simple practices that create steadiness, so your finances support your health, your impact and your future.

What we'll do here:

- Reframe abundance as an inner state that guides outer decisions.
- Clarify values-based spending (what actually matters).
- Build practical stability (buffers, cash flow, clean debt, simple investing).
- Create a money rhythm you can stick to without overwhelm.

Abundance — The Inner Foundation of Wealth

Abundance begins before the numbers: in the beliefs you hold, the safety you feel and the alignment between your values and your choices. From that grounded place, the practical steps become simple and sustainable.

When I truly grasped the idea that there is enough for everyone, something in me shifted. I was changed, forever. I dropped my ego, and with it, the pressure to compete. I stopped seeing others as rivals and started seeing them as reminders of what's possible.

Letting go of a scarcity or victim mindset changes everything. The world looks different. It feels lighter. Brighter. More expansive.

And when you feel good, and focus on the right things, positive things begin to flow in ways you never expected.

Having an abundance mentality isn't about being greedy. And it's definitely not about believing you have to work yourself to the bone to deserve good things in life.

Abundance is a mindset grounded in the belief that there's enough for everyone. When we let go of ego, resistance and limiting self-beliefs, life begins to unfold with more ease. It's not magic; it's alignment.

Many of my clients grew up in environments where life was tough. Money was a source of stress. They watched their parents struggle to make ends meet, and as a result, they unconsciously formed the belief that money is scarce and that only relentless hard work makes you worthy of having it.

Now, there's nothing wrong with hard work. In fact, it's a key ingredient in the *Balanced Success* recipe. But without addressing our underlying beliefs, we often self-sabotage just before the breakthrough.

Research backs this up. Studies show that people who adopt an abundance mindset, one rooted in gratitude, visualisation and positive self-talk, tend to make more confident and consistent financial decisions. One recent study found that 59% of people who regularly visualised their financial goals reported increased confidence, compared to just 31% who didn't.

This isn't just about manifesting; it's about psychology. The way we think about money shapes how we feel, and that emotional state directly impacts the actions we take (or avoid). Over time, those small actions form patterns and those patterns shape our financial reality.

This chapter is an invitation to explore your relationship with money, not just practically, but personally and emotionally. Because abundance doesn't begin in your bank account. It starts in your mind, your beliefs and your energy.

Before we move to the practical side of finance, take a moment to reflect on this simple but powerful comparison:

Abundance Mindset	Scarcity Mindset
Enough for everyone	Zero-sum
Gratitude	Fear
Invest and grow	Hoard
Share Wins	Jealous
Collaborative	Competitive

Understanding the Mindset Shift

The purpose of this comparison isn't to judge where you currently sit; it's to raise awareness. Most people move between both mindsets depending on their circumstances, stress levels or past experiences. The power comes in recognising when you're operating from scarcity, and consciously choosing to shift into abundance.

> An abundance mindset doesn't mean ignoring challenges. It means trusting that you can meet those challenges with resourcefulness, optimism, and a belief that you are supported.

It's about possibility over panic, curiosity over control, and expansiveness over fear.

Start noticing your language. Are you saying things like:
- *There's never enough.*
- *I could never afford that.*
- *That's just not realistic for me.*

Or are you shifting into statements like:
- *I'm open to new opportunities.*
- *There's always another way.*
- *I trust that what I need will find me.*

When you begin to embody the energy of abundance, your decisions change. Your leadership changes. And most importantly, your lived experience changes.

From here, we transition into the practical side of building wealth—the tools, habits and strategies that allow abundance to become reality.

Money as Energy, Not Just Math

For years, I told myself I wasn't "a numbers person". I could build a business plan, sure. But when it came to my personal finances or truly understanding the deeper layers of profit and cash flow in my business, I would often handball it off or avoid it altogether.

Why? Because money held emotional weight. It felt hard, heavy or confronting. And for many people I work with, it's the same.

Money is never just about money. It's about stories. The ones we inherited. The ones we're still telling ourselves.

But here's what I've learned: when you shift your perspective and see money as a tool, not a threat, everything changes. You stop avoiding it. You start partnering with it. You make clearer, calmer decisions. You align your finances with your values. And that is powerful.

Financial Literacy is Self-Leadership

You don't need to become an accountant. But you do need to become literate. Especially if you're leading a business, a family or even just your own life.

Basic financial fluency is an act of self-respect. It's not boring. It's empowering.

Here are a few foundations I believe every leader should know:
- The difference between profit and revenue.
- How to read a simple P&L (Profit and Loss Statement).
- What cash flow really means.
- The power of compound interest.
- What debt is costing you (and how to manage it wisely).
- The importance of an emergency fund.
- Aligning your budget with your values.
- When you understand your numbers, you stop guessing. You start leading with clarity. That's what creates financial peace.

The Cost of Financial Avoidance

Most people don't avoid money because they're lazy. They avoid it because it feels confronting. Maybe it triggers shame. Or past trauma. Or fear of being judged.

But avoidance comes at a cost. It creates stress that lingers under the surface. It keeps you in a loop of reacting instead of leading. It erodes your sense of control.

In my coaching work, I've seen what happens when people stop looking the other way. Even just one small habit change—checking your bank account weekly, reviewing your expenses, or having an honest money conversation—can build momentum.

Financial empowerment is a key part of *Balanced Success*. When you feel safe, supported and clear with money, your nervous system calms. Your decision-making sharpens. Your leadership expands.

Money Stories and Identity

Ask yourself: *What did I learn about money growing up?*

Was it talked about? Avoided? Used as a reward or punishment? Were there beliefs like *you have to work hard for every dollar*, or *rich people are greedy*?

So much of our adult behaviour with money is shaped by childhood conditioning. But here's the good news: you're not stuck with those beliefs. You can rewrite them. You can choose new ones.

That's what abundance is. It's not just about having more; it's about feeling free and resourced from within. It's trusting that there's enough. That *you* are enough.

Build a Conscious Financial Plan

Financial planning doesn't have to be dry. It can be deeply values-based. Start by asking:
- *What does "enough" mean to me?*
- *What kind of lifestyle do I actually want to create?*
- *Where am I spending out of habit, and where am I spending from alignment?*

A conscious financial plan is one that supports your goals *and* your wellbeing. It gives you room to breathe. To save. To give. To enjoy.

You can build a business that's profitable and ethical. You can grow wealth in a way that feels nourishing, not depleting. You can create a life where money supports your values instead of overriding them.

This is what *Balanced Success* looks like. And it starts with clarity, courage and a willingness to look at money with new eyes.

Key Messages: Abundance & Finance

- Money is neutral; alignment gives it purpose.
- Clarity first: know income, expenses, cash flow.

BALANCED SUCCESS

- Define "enough" and spend to your values.
- Build buffers: automate saving and safety nets.
- Reduce debt; keep cash flow clean.
- Keep it simple: consistent investing beats complexity.
- Stop avoidance: small steps weekly (money date).
- Let money fund wellbeing, impact and freedom.

Balanced Success Check-In — Abundance & Finance

Instructions

How to Complete This Check-In

1. **Rate each area (1–10).**
   1 = off-track/struggling, 5 = mixed/variable,
   10 = thriving/consistent.
2. **Add quick notes.**
   In "Notes or Reflections", capture wins, friction points, patterns, triggers, or context (e.g., travel, deadlines).
3. **Choose one tiny upgrade.**
   Pick **one** specific, low-effort change for the next seven days.
   Aim to "make the good choice the easy choice".

- Clarity (I know my numbers today):
- Cash flow clean (income minus expenses):
- Safety buffer active:
- Values-aligned spending:
- Momentum (debt plan or investing habit)

Reflect (1–2 lines):

- My biggest money stress this week is:
- "Enough" for this month looks like:

🏃 Tiny action (choose one):
- Raise my auto-savings by 1–2%.
- Move $___ to the buffer.
- Cancel one unused subscription.
- List debts + interest rates.
- Schedule a 20 minute "money date" with yourself, or with a finance specialist.
- Identify one value-aligned cut and one keep.

Commit (one line):

This week I will strengthen my finances by:

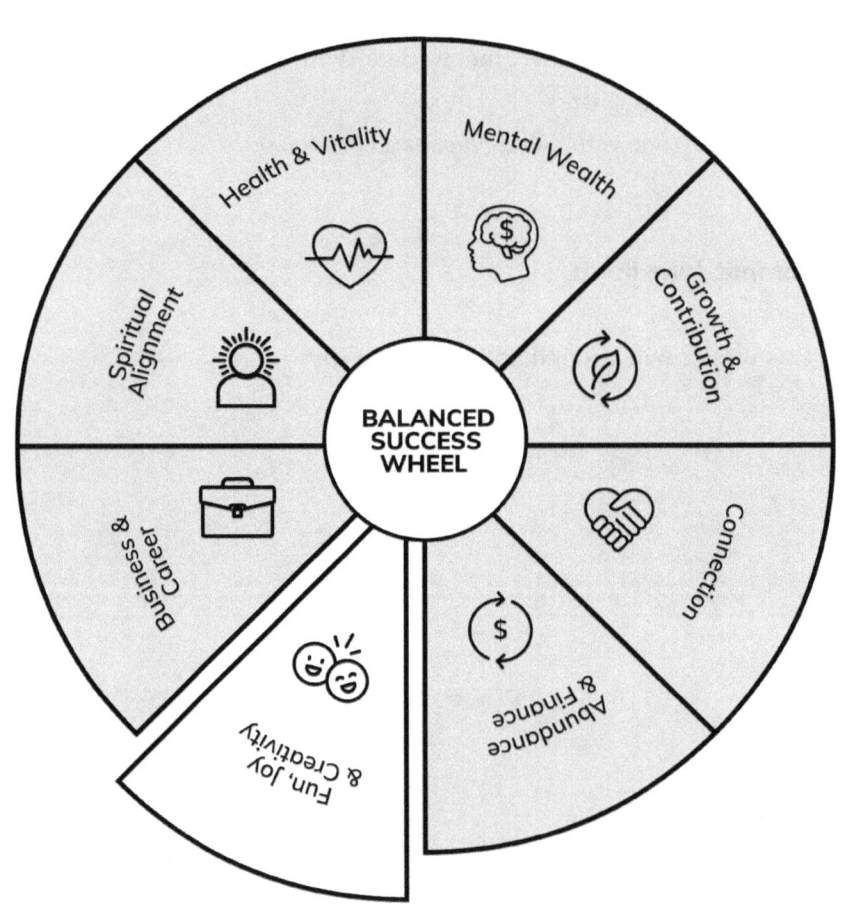

CHAPTER TEN

Fun, Joy & Creativity

Life is here to be enjoyed. Without joy, life can begin to feel heavy, dull and disconnected. Joy isn't just for holidays or special occasions; it's a way of living. A mindset. A gentle practice of seeking lightness in our day-to-day. It's what lifts the ordinary into something memorable.

It might be…listening to your favourite music on the train,

dancing while you clean the house,

playing a board game with a friend,

or cooking your favourite meal with love.

Of course, there will be times where we feel low, sad or stressed. That is part of life for everyone. These situations are important, as they provide a contrast for our emotions, so when we get back to feeling joy, we appreciate it so much more.

Imagine if you lived in a utopia where everything was perfect. After a while, you would stop feeling joy, because if joy was the only emotion you felt all day, you would eventually get bored.

Joy is a deep, soul-level emotion; a sense of lightness, presence and connection that often arises spontaneously, not because everything is perfect, but because something within you feels aligned, whole and awake in the moment.

While happiness is often tied to external circumstances (a promotion, a holiday, a compliment), joy is more internal. It's a state of being; a feeling that can rise up even in the midst of difficulty. You might feel joy when:

- Watching your child laugh uncontrollably.
- Feeling the sun on your face after a storm.
- Creating something meaningful.
- Being fully present with someone you love.
- Realising you're exactly where you're meant to be.

According to the Merriam-Webster Dictionary, joy is "the emotion evoked by well-being, success, or good fortune or by the prospect of possessing what one desires".

Brené Brown describes joy as a form of spiritual connection and gratitude that often surprises us. She believes joy is the most vulnerable emotion we experience because we're so afraid it won't last.

In the context of *Balanced Success*, joy can be seen as:

A compass, not the destination, but a signal that you are living in alignment with your truth.

Joy doesn't require perfection, it just requires presence, connection and often, a sense of purpose.

From Joy to Fun: The Lighter Side of Living

While joy is often quiet, internal and soul-deep, fun is more external, active and energising. Fun is the spark that brings joy to life in motion. It's the dance party in the kitchen, the spontaneous road trip, the belly laugh that catches you off guard.

Joy is the compass...but fun is the adventure.

As a mum of two children under 10, a partner and a business owner, life is full-on. The majority of my time is spent within my top three core values: love, vitality and empowerment. And while those are deeply fulfilling, it's easy to fall into a mindset where there's no energy left for anything else.

That's why I make a conscious decision to prioritise fun.

For me, that usually looks like a date night out at least once a month, lunch with a good friend or going to a live music gig. It shouldn't be an optional extra, even when life is full. Fun should be a non-negotiable.

Engaging in fun activities often leads to laughter and smiling, which are not just enjoyable but also physiologically beneficial. Laughter has been shown to trigger the release of several neurochemicals, including dopamine, serotonin, endorphins and oxytocin, all of which help regulate mood, reduce stress, boost immunity and promote social bonding.

Research from the Mayo Clinic (Dunbar et al, 2012) and other peer-reviewed studies confirms that laughter activates the brain's reward system, reducing cortisol levels and improving overall emotional well-being.

Now here's something I want you to consider:

When was the last time you did something really different, just for fun?

Sometimes we get so stuck in routines that we default to the same things over and over—the same places, the same people, the same conversations. It can feel comforting…until it gets boring. What used to be fun starts to feel flat.

That's why I recommend building *variety* into your fun time. Try something new. Think outside the box. I'm not saying you have to trek through the Amazon, but hey, if that speaks to you, go for it!

Often, creating new experiences requires stepping outside your comfort zone. You may have to push yourself. But when you do, you'll likely feel that spark again; that sense of exhilaration that reminds you that you're *alive*.

Life is here to be explored. Don't fall victim to old ways of doing things.

Change it up. Live fully. Have more fun.

A Fun Brainstorming Session

Here's a light-hearted and expansive exercise to spark inspiration and reconnect you with your playful side.

Find a relaxed space, somewhere you feel calm, open and free from distractions. Give yourself permission to dream without limits. The goal is not perfection, it's possibility.

Fill out the two columns with as many ideas as you can think of. They don't need to be extravagant or expensive, just experiences and adventures that light you up.

Once you've completed your list, consider sharing it with a close friend, partner or even your kids. You might be surprised at the conversations it sparks and how contagious inspiration can be.

Fun Brainstorm

Places You Want to Visit

Things You Want to Do

Places You Want to Visit	Things You Want to Do
Greece (Islands & Culture)	Take a cooking class - cuisine
Uluru, NT	Go horseback riding on the beach
Tasmania (road trip and hiking)	Learn to cook
Broome and Cable Beach	Ride Camels
Japan in Cherry Blossom Season	Hike a multi-day trail
Queenstown, New Zealand	Go skydiving or hot air ballooning
Byron Bay (Wellness Retreat)	Try paddleboarding
Norway to see the Northern Lights	Take a digial detox weekend
The Great Barrier Reef	Learn to scuba dive
Paris in spring	Write a poem
Bali (silent retreat)	Learn to surf
Iceland (glacier lagoons)	Start a creative side project
New York City (for the buzz)	Go on spontaneous weekend away
Margaret River (wine & coast)	Learn a new musical instrument
Florence and the Italian countryroad	Host a themed dinner party

Now it's your turn

Places You Want to Visit

Things You Want to Do

BALANCED SUCCESS

I hope that exercise got you thinking about how much more there is to experience and enjoy in this life. Don't put it off for "someday"; that day may never come. Fun, like joy, isn't a luxury; it's a vital ingredient in a fulfilling, balanced life.

> *"We don't stop playing because we grow old;*
> *we grow old because we stop playing."*
> **– George Bernard Shaw, playwright and critic**

And speaking of play, it's also the birthplace of creativity. When we give ourselves permission to have fun, explore and try new things, we unlock the kind of thinking that leads to innovation, fresh ideas and deeper self-expression. Let's explore how creativity fits into your version of *Balanced Success*.

Creativity: Play as a Pathway

When I was young, I loved drawing, writing poems and making up games in nature. Somewhere along the way, though, I forgot how creative I really am. I even remember saying to people, more than once, *I'm just not a creative person.*

I had spent so many years focused on building strategies, writing business plans, running agendas and analysing spreadsheets, that the creative parts of me were buried so deep I'd completely forgotten they were there.

It wasn't until my Mum handed me a few poems I'd written when I was 10 years old that something shifted. I didn't even believe they were mine at first! But there they were— raw, rhythmic and full of feeling. That moment cracked something open in me. It reminded me that creativity was never gone, it was just waiting patiently to be invited back.

What is Creativity?

Creativity isn't limited to painting or poetry. It's the act of bringing something into existence that didn't exist before, such as a fresh idea, a new solution, an unexpected connection or a piece of art.

At its core, creativity is self-expression. It's letting your imagination stretch beyond logic. It's experimenting, exploring and making something with heart.

Creativity might look like:
- Brainstorming new business ideas.
- Cooking a meal without a recipe.
- Writing in a journal.
- Styling an outfit.
- Designing a workshop.
- Building a sandcastle with your kids.

It's not about being "good" at something, it's about allowing yourself to create, just for the sake of creating.

We Are All Creative

Every single human being is born creative. We're wired for it. You only have to look at children to see this in action; they imagine, pretend, build and play without hesitation.

But somewhere along the way, many of us unlearn our creativity. We're told to be practical, productive, efficient. We swap crayons for calculators. We trade curiosity for conformity.

The truth? Your creativity never left you, it just got quiet.

You don't have to become an artist to reclaim it. You just have to give yourself permission to explore without pressure. To make something simply because it brings you joy.

Why Creativity is Important

Reconnecting with your creativity isn't just fun, it's essential for balanced success.

Creativity helps you to:
- Think differently and solve problems with innovation.
- Stay mentally flexible and emotionally open.
- Process emotions and tap into self-awareness.
- Reduce stress and feel more alive.
- Lead your business with vision, not just systems.

In fact, studies show that engaging in creative activities can reduce anxiety, improve mood and even strengthen neural pathways in the brain.

Creativity is medicine, and as leaders, it helps us access a deeper kind of intelligence: intuitive, expansive and alive.

Simple Ideas to Embrace Your Creative Side

You don't need hours of free time or fancy materials. Here are a few easy ways to invite creativity back into your world:
- Keep a small notebook with you and jot down thoughts, lyrics, ideas or doodles.
- Play music and let yourself move or dance without a plan.
- Visit a gallery, museum or local market for inspiration.
- Cook a meal with ingredients you've never used before.
- Try your hand at watercolours, clay or a simple DIY project.
- Write freely in a journal for 10 minutes each day without editing.
- Play "what if" games with your kids or partner. Let your imagination run wild.
- Decorate a space in your home to reflect your style and mood.
- Create a vision board using magazines, quotes and images that speak to your soul.

Final Thoughts: Your Life Is Meant to Be Lived Fully

Joy, fun and creativity aren't distractions from success; they are part of what makes success truly fulfilling. They recharge your energy, expand your mind and reconnect you with the parts of yourself that may have been buried under pressure and responsibility.

If you've been waiting for the right moment to bring more lightness into your life, this is your invitation.

Start small. Start now.

Take a moment today to do something just because it brings you joy. Try something new for the fun of it. Make space for creativity, not because you have to, but because it's who you are.

Key Messages: Joy, Fun & Creativity

- Joy is fuel, not a luxury.
- Fun regulates your nervous system.
- Creativity grows when you give it space.
- Schedule joy the way you schedule work.
- Protect play time from distractions.
- Move your body to lift your mood and ideas.
- Curate inputs that spark curiosity.
- Practise small daily acts of creativity.
- Share joy with others to deepen connection.
- Use joy as a reset when stress rises.
- Track what activities actually light you up.
- Review each season: keep what brings energy, drop what drains it.

Balanced Success Check-In: Joy, Fun & Creativity

Instructions

- **Rate each line (1–10)** in the blank.
  1–3 = off-track, 4–6 = building, 7–8 = consistent, 9–10 = integrated.
- **Add one quick note** beside any line (e.g., an example, friction point, or win).
- **Choose one small action** for the lowest-scoring line for the next seven days.
- **Joy**. How often do you feel present, grateful, and light-hearted?

- **Fun**. How regularly do you do things that energise you and make you laugh?
- **Creativity**. How connected do you feel to your imagination and self-expression?

What's one small action you can take this week to lift one of these scores?

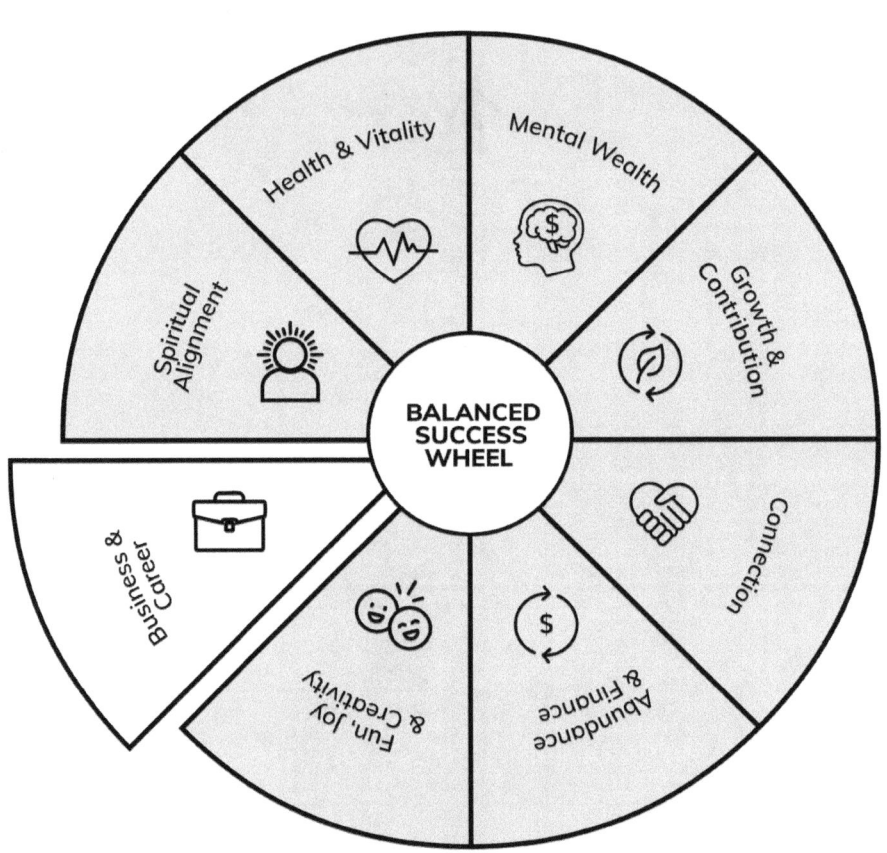

CHAPTER ELEVEN
Business & Career

Everything is changing in the world of business and careers; we are living through one of the most significant transformations of our time. The job market is being reshaped rapidly, and AI is at the centre of that shift. According to the University of Sydney's *Skills Horizon 2025* report, automation and AI are driving a dramatic overhaul of traditional roles, tasks and skills. Industries are transforming. Entire job categories are being redefined. And what's valued in leadership is evolving, fast.

Companies are racing to redesign their business models to remain competitive. This has massive implications for leaders, who are now required to adapt, grow and take action at a much faster pace than ever before. In the context of *Balanced Success*, this chapter will help you gain perspective, anchor into your personal leadership values and build mental wealth to thrive through change.

Navigating the Transition

The *Skills Horizon* 2025 report outlines five key disruptive shifts shaping the future of leadership:

1. **Technology and AI Fluency** — Leaders need to understand and integrate AI into their strategy and operations, not as a threat, but as an advantage.
2. **Values-Based Leadership** — Organisations are increasingly judged by their ethics, transparency and societal impact. Leaders must embody these values.
3. **Radical Accountability** — Performance and culture metrics are now more visible and measurable. Leaders must take ownership beyond just profits.
4. **Trust and Transparency** — In a world of misinformation, authenticity and communication are everything. People follow leaders they trust.
5. **Energy and Mental Wealth** — Sustainable leadership requires more than performance — it requires maintaining your energy, inner clarity and emotional wellbeing.

These aren't just "nice-to-haves"; they are essential for future leadership. And they're directly aligned with the principles of *Balanced Success*. The report also highlighted a rise in demand for mental wealth—the combination of mental wellbeing, self-awareness and leadership resilience. In a high-change environment, the ability to self-regulate, connect with purpose and stay mentally clear is becoming just as valuable as strategic thinking.

Make AI Work With You, Not Against You

In a world saturated with AI tools and automation, it's easy to feel like you're falling behind. But here's the empowering truth: you don't need to be a tech expert to lead in an AI world, you just need to stay curious and adaptable.

Balanced Success isn't about resisting innovation; it's about leveraging it in a way that aligns with your values, strengths and team culture. You can start small:

- Use AI to automate repetitive admin so you can focus on what matters most.
- Explore tools that support creativity, communication or wellbeing in your business.
- Empower your team to experiment with AI, rather than fear it, creating a culture of learning and curiosity.

One of the core principles of *mental wealth* is staying in control of your energy and focus. If you're using tech reactively (trying to do more, faster), you'll likely end up depleted. But if you use it intentionally, to support clarity, alignment and flow, it becomes a powerful enabler of the *Balanced Success* life.

Leading with Conscious Awareness in a Technological Age

With all this change, it's easy to get swept up in the need to "keep up", But here's the truth: if leaders don't ground themselves in conscious awareness, they risk becoming reactive, burned out or irrelevant.

This era isn't just about knowing what to do with AI. It's about knowing who you are as a leader. It's about staying anchored in your values, leading with emotional intelligence and making decisions from clarity, not fear.

The leaders of the future are not just tech-savvy; they are self-aware, purpose-driven and values-aligned. They don't just know how to use

The Leader Who Almost Missed the Shift

One of my clients—let's call her Michelle—ran a successful mid-sized consulting firm. She'd been in the game for over 15 years and was proud of her strong team culture and solid revenue.

But over the past year, things started to feel…off. Recruitment was harder. Some of her long-standing clients weren't renewing. Her younger team members were disengaging.

At first, she doubled down on what had always worked—tighter KPIs, more structure, clearer delivery frameworks. But nothing changed.

When she came to coaching with me, she was exhausted. What we uncovered was this: the world around her business had changed, but her leadership style hadn't. She hadn't made time to consider where her team needed to go, emotionally, technologically or strategically. She wasn't resisting AI, but she wasn't embracing it either.

Through our work together, she made some big shifts. She redesigned her operating model, started hosting monthly team innovation labs and brought in AI-powered tools to support workflow, not to replace people, but to free them up. Most importantly, she did her own personal alignment work and reconnected with her role as a conscious leader.

Six months later, her business was back on track. But more than that—her team was energised. She wasn't just surviving the change; she was leading it. Her clarity, energy and presence had returned, and with it, the foundation of mental wealth.

What If You're Ready for a Career Change?

Now, some of you might be reading this and thinking: *That sounds great, but what if I don't want to lead the same business? What if I'm ready to pivot completely?*

That's valid. The world of work is changing so fast that many people are feeling called to reinvent themselves. And that's not something to fear, it's something to explore.

- *What do I want to contribute in this next chapter of my life?*
- *Which parts of my career no longer feel aligned?*
- *Where am I resisting change, and what would happen if I leaned in instead?*

You don't have to burn it all down to make a change. Start small. Take one step toward something that excites you. Learn about emerging industries. Have coffee with someone in a field you're curious about. The path to reinvention doesn't start with a resume; it starts with a decision to live in alignment.

This is not just a time of disruption, it's a time of immense possibility. And the leaders who thrive will be the ones who align with it from the inside out, building clarity, emotional capacity and mental wealth along the way.

 Key Messages:

- We are living through a major transformation in the job market, driven by AI and automation.
- Leadership is being redefined; success now requires mental wealth, emotional intelligence and adaptability.
- The *Skills Horizon 2025* report outlines five key shifts every leader must embrace.
- Conscious, values-led leadership is not optional, it's essential.
- Reinvention is not failure. It's alignment.
  And it begins from within.

BALANCED SUCCESS

Balanced Success Check-In – Business & Career

On a scale of 1–10, with one being "not at all aligned" and 10 being "completely aligned", how aligned do you feel in your current work or business?

What's energising you, and what's draining you?

What's one action you can take this month to move toward more aligned, future-ready leadership?

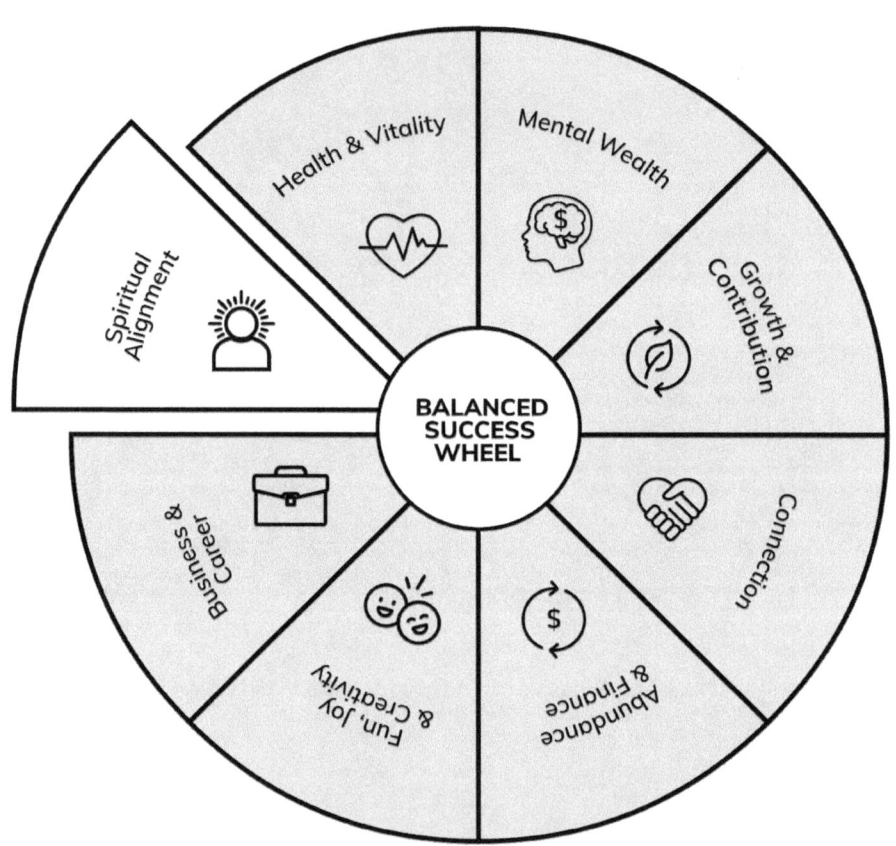

CHAPTER TWELVE
Spiritual Alignment

We live in a world that teaches us to seek success externally—to climb, achieve, hustle and build. And while these things matter, they're not the full picture. Because true fulfilment doesn't come from what you *do*, it comes from who you *are* while you're doing it.

That's what this chapter is about.

Spiritual alignment is the deepest kind of alignment. It's the place where your inner truth, intuition and energy meet. It's what anchors you when everything else changes. It's the voice that whispers when the world gets loud. It's the knowing that you are not separate; you are part of something much greater.

BALANCED SUCCESS

This isn't about religion or dogma. You don't need crystals, mantras, or a guru.

What you need is connection—to your inner self, to the universe, to the quiet intelligence that exists beneath the surface of everyday life.

Some people call it Source. Others call it God, the Universe, Energy, or Consciousness. The name doesn't matter. The experience does.

When we're spiritually aligned, life feels clearer. Decisions become easier. We attract more of what we want and repel what no longer serves us. We feel less reactive and more at peace. And in moments of uncertainty or challenge, we don't crumble; we *remember* who we are.

But when we're disconnected, when we live only from the mind and ignore the whispers of the soul, we burn out. We force. We strive. We numb. And eventually, we lose touch with our purpose, no matter how "successful" our lives look from the outside.

I didn't realise how disconnected I had become until everything familiar was stripped away.

Tanya's Story: Waking Up in TriBeCa

About a year into living in TriBeCa, NYC, after the adrenaline had faded and the chaos of change had finally settled, I woke up one morning and felt…different.

I had made massive life shifts in a short space of time. I'd uprooted my life, moved across the world, left my family and friends behind, started a new company and immersed myself in the culture of Manhattan. Everything was different to how it had been before: where I lived, the people I surrounded myself with, how I worked, even how I spent my weekends.

The dramatic change stripped away everything familiar. There were no external reference points—no routines, no expectations, no comforting patterns. And in that space of unfamiliarity, something new had room to surface.

It is hard to pinpoint what prompted my thoughts on that morning in TriBeCa. But somehow, the world looked different. It *felt* different. And I realised: *I was different.*

At first, it was disorienting, like I no longer fit the version of myself I had brought with me. But as the discomfort softened, curiosity took over. I became obsessed with learning, about consciousness, energy, healing, intuition and the unseen forces that shape our lives.

I realised there was more to this world than what we see. And more to success than what we're taught.

I began to understand that energy—subtle, intelligent, and invisible—plays a central role in everything. Not just in health, but in relationships, decision-making, creativity and leadership. When we align with that energy, life begins to move with more ease and meaning. When we don't, it feels forced and fragmented.

That moment was my first experience of true spiritual alignment. It wasn't something I found in a book or a workshop. It was something that revealed itself through change, discomfort, and ultimately stillness.

Signs You're Spiritually Disconnected

Spiritual misalignment doesn't always scream. More often, it whispers; quiet discomforts that accumulate until something feels off.
- Constant overthinking. The mind runs the show. You spin in circles, unable to land.
- Decision paralysis. Even simple choices feel overwhelming. Logic offers no clarity.

- Feeling stuck (even when everything "should" be good). You've achieved the goals but still feel disconnected. It's the *is this all there is?* feeling.
- Loss of joy and synchronicity. Life becomes heavy. The sparkle fades. Coincidences and flow stop appearing.
- Disconnection from intuition. You override your gut. You stop listening to your inner wisdom.

These aren't failures. They're signals. As Dr. Mihaly Csikszentmihalyi's research in *Flow* (2022) shows, disconnection from meaning and presence often leads to anxiety, burnout and restlessness. Flow theory argues that when we are absolutely focused and engaged in the present moment, we are in a state of flow and, therefore, intrinsically motivated.

Core Practices for Spiritual Alignment

You don't need to change your entire life to reconnect spiritually. But you do need to slow down long enough to hear your own truth again.

Meditation and Stillness

Regular stillness trains you to observe, not react. It opens space for clarity, intuition, and peace. A 2021 *Frontiers in Psychology* study found mindfulness significantly enhances emotional regulation and cognitive flexibility, both vital for aligned leadership.

Intuition as Data

Intuition isn't fluffy, it's *fast-tracked internal wisdom*. The Academy of Management Perspectives suggests that seasoned leaders rely on subconscious pattern recognition, what we often call a "gut feeling", as a key decision-making tool.

Journaling for Inner Truth

Journaling helps unearth clarity buried under busyness. Try prompts like:
What am I ignoring?
What does my intuition already know?

Visualisation (Inspired by Joe Dispenza)

Dr Joe Dispenza's research shows that mentally rehearsing your future, with elevated emotion, rewires the brain as if it's already happening. It aligns your thoughts and energy toward the life you're creating.

Feeling Your Way Forward

Sometimes, the body knows before the mind does. Listen to the pull. Trust the nudge. Feeling is one of your most accurate forms of intelligence.

For Leaders at a Crossroads – Contribution from Sonja Kay, Tanya's spiritual mentor

When your work begins to feel empty, even when it "should" feel fulfilling, it is not a flaw. It is a call to pause. To take timeout. To question. To realign.

This kind of inner discomfort is not something to push through. It is sacred intelligence, your soul's way of saying the version of success you have been chasing no longer fits who you are becoming.

You have outgrown the story.

When purpose starts to fade and achievement no longer fuels you, it is a sign you are ready to lead from a deeper place, not just with strategy, but with soul. These moments of questioning are not the end. They are the threshold to you evolving into parts of yourself you have never seen before.

The Link Between Spirituality and Leadership

In a data-driven world, intuitive leaders stand out, not because they abandon logic, but because they integrate it with deeper knowing.

- Inner Alignment = Outer Clarity. When you're grounded in your values and inner truth, your decisions feel calm, even if they're bold.
- Intuition Strengthens Strategy. Research shows intuitive intelligence can reduce decision fatigue and increase leadership confidence in complex environments.
- Legacy Over Ego. The best leaders aren't just tactical, they're soulful. They lead with purpose, and that energy creates trust, longevity and impact.

As the HeartMath Institute's work shows, heart-brain coherence enhances not just personal health, but leadership presence and decision-making too.

Key Messages: Spiritual Alignment

- Spiritual alignment is personal and practical.
- Quiet the noise so you can hear your inner guidance.
- Intuition is a tool. Ask, listen, act, reflect.
- Values and boundaries protect your energy.
- Presence over perfection.
- Choose simple practices that fit you: meditation, breath, nature, gratitude.
- Notice signals of alignment: calm, clarity, flow. Notice misalignment: heaviness, resistance.
- Create small rituals morning and night.
- Curate your inputs. What you consume shapes how you feel.
- Let purpose guide service and contribution.

 **Reflections + Practices**

Journal Prompts:
When do I feel most connected to something greater than myself?
What do I trust, deep down, that logic can't explain?
Where have I been guided before—through intuition, signs, or synchronicity?
What practices help me feel most aligned?
What might the universe be showing me right now?

Balanced Success Check-In – Spiritual Alignment

Instructions

1. **Rate each line (1–10)** in the blank.
   1–3 = off-track, 4–6 = building, 7–8 = consistent, 9–10 = integrated.
2. **Add one quick note** beside any line (e.g., an example, friction point, or win).
3. **Choose one small action** for the lowest-scoring line for the next seven days.
- Inner stillness today: __
- Intuition consulted before action: __
- Values-aligned choices: __
- Boundaries respected: __
- Sense of connection and purpose: __

BALANCED SUCCESS

🏃 **Tiny action (choose one):**

- Two minutes of slow breathing.
- Barefoot grounding for five minutes.
- One line of gratitude.
- Ask for guidance, listen for one minute.
- Turn off one noisy input for an hour.

Commit (one line):

Awareness is the gateway to alignment. You don't need to fix everything overnight. You just need to start listening again.

CHAPTER THIRTEEN:
Balanced Success Life – Taking Action

"The secret of your future is hidden in your daily routine."
— **Mike Murdock, songwriter, pastor**

Hopefully by now you've read all the chapters that make up the *Balanced Success* recipe. If not, I encourage you to go back, even if a topic feels familiar. Sometimes, it's the chapters we think we already know that hold the biggest breakthroughs.

The *Balanced Success* model was designed to highlight the key ingredients that contribute to a life that's aligned, fulfilling and sustainable. But remember: this model is a starting point, not a prescription. You're encouraged to personalise it. If there are areas you'd like to add, remove, or rename, do it. This is your life. Your version of success.

To help you reflect, a blank *Balanced Success Wheel* has been included on page 193. Use it to create your own version based on what truly matters to you.

From Insight to Action: Building Your Personal System

Reading and reflecting is powerful. But transformation happens when we take action, and stick with it. That means building systems that support the life you want to live.

Let's be honest: motivation fades. Willpower isn't sustainable. What creates long-term change is having a system. As James Clear writes in *Atomic Habits* (2018, 2024), "You do not rise to the level of your goals. You fall to the level of your systems."

This chapter will guide you through a simple, effective process to implement what you've learned so far.

Step 1: Create Your Final Baseline

Use the *Balanced Success Wheel* below. For each area of your life, go back through the relevant chapter and reflect on your current reality. Give yourself a score from 1 to 10 for each segment.

Once you've scored each area, write the number on the wheel and shade in the segment to represent where you are now. This is your starting point; your final baseline before realignment.

BALANCED SUCCESS

Your Scores:

Area	My Score (1–10)	Notes
Chapter 5		
Health and Vitality - Nutrition		
Health and Vitality – Sleep & Relaxation		
Health and Vitality – Exercise		
Health and Vitality – Eliminating Toxins		
Chapter 6		
Mental Wealth - Purpose		
Mental Wealth - Values		
Mental Wealth - Resilience		
Mental Wealth - Clarity		
Mental Wealth - Self-Awareness		
Mental Wealth - Habits		
Chapter 7		
Growth & Contribution		
Chapter 8		
Connection		
Chapter 9		
Abundance & Finance		
Chapter 10		
Fun, Joy & Creativity		
Chapter 11		
Business & Career		
Chapter 12		
Spiritual Alignment		

This simple list will help you see where your biggest gaps are and where to focus your energy first.

Now that you've scored all areas, list them from lowest to highest:

Step 2: Choose 1–3 Focus Areas

While all the areas are important, trying to tackle everything at once will only lead to overwhelm. Instead, start small.

Choose 1–3 areas that:
- Scored the lowest.
- Feel most urgent.
- Would create momentum if improved.

Focus on those for the next 90 days.

Remember: if you improve by just 1% each day, you'll be 37 times better over the course of a year. This principle is known as the power of marginal gains, a concept made popular by James Clear. Just like compound interest in finance, small improvements in your habits can lead to massive transformation.

> *"Habits are the compound interest of self-improvement."*
> **— James Clear**

The idea is simple: consistent, incremental progress adds up. You don't need to make huge changes all at once. Instead, make small intentional improvements, and allow those to compound over time. This is how *Balanced Success* becomes not just a concept, but a lifestyle.

Step 3: Design Your Realignment Routine

Use the following prompts to create a simple routine that keeps you aligned:

- **Morning Rituals**: How can you start the day with intention?
- **Weekly Review**: Set a time to reflect on your wheel scores and any shifts.
- **90-Day Check-In**: Re-do your wheel and note changes in each area.

You may also wish to:

- Use a journal or planner.
- Use a coach.
- Share your goals with a mentor or accountability partner.

Set Yourself Up for Success

While personal reflection is powerful, the journey of *Balanced Success* becomes even more impactful when it's shared.

Consider inviting a friend, family member, or coach to join you. Having someone to check in with, celebrate wins and hold space for your realignment journey can make all the difference. Accountability creates momentum and shared growth creates deeper connection.

And don't forget to make it fun.

This is your life. It's not a punishment, it's a privilege to shape. So enjoy creating it with intention. Play with new habits. Experiment with your routines. Celebrate progress, not perfection. This is your season to build something beautiful, on your terms.

Balanced Success Action Checklist

Use this checklist to help you implement the *Balanced Success* model with clarity and consistency:

- *Reflect*
- *Establish Your Baseline*
- *Prioritise*

- *Systemise and Simplify*
- *Build Support*
- *Celebrate Progress*

Balanced Success is built one intentional choice at a time. Keep going. You're creating something meaningful.

Balanced Success isn't a finish line. It's a practice. A way of life.

It's about tuning into what matters. Taking action with intention. Adjusting when you drift. And showing up, again and again, for the life you want to lead.

You have everything you need within you.

Now it's time to begin.

The Parts We Avoid – What Neglect Reveals About Us

"We avoid the parts of life that threaten the stories we tell ourselves."
— Coach Hudson, executive coach and leadership psychologist

Everyone does it. Even the most successful, self-aware and high-functioning people have blind spots. Areas they neglect, avoid or put in the "later" basket. Whether it's health, finances, rest, relationships or purpose, there's usually at least one area we'd rather not look at too closely.

Why? Because avoidance isn't about laziness. It's about protection.

We avoid the things that feel emotionally loaded, confusing or vulnerable. Often, these are areas that hold unresolved pain; pain that originated in a specific moment, relationship or belief from our past. According to leadership psychologist Coach Hudson, "Avoidance is rarely about the surface task. It's about the meaning we've attached to that area, often unconsciously."

Why We Avoid

Avoidance shows up in different ways for different people. It might be:
- Avoiding your finances because money was always a source of stress or shame growing up.
- Ignoring your health because you don't want to confront the habits you've formed.
- Numbing your need for rest because your worth has always been tied to productivity.
- Neglecting creativity because you were told your ideas weren't valuable.

Whatever the pattern, the impact is the same: misalignment. And over time, that misalignment compounds. Avoidance creates blind spots. And blind spots erode trust, not just with others, but within yourself.

Digging Without Clarity

Clarity is an area I avoided for a very long time. I spent years upon years being busy and immersing myself in the "doing". I had dug a hole so deep I couldn't even see the surface. My mind and body were not connected, and I was covered in a deep fog. I had no sense of who I was, what I was doing, or why.

Looking back, I can see that I was terrified to stop digging. Stillness felt dangerous. Because stillness, over time, would reveal the truth: *I was deeply unhappy, completely unaligned with my soul, and utterly lost.*

Avoidance had become a survival strategy. But it was also slowly costing me my clarity, my vitality and my truth.

What Neglect Reveals

The areas we avoid are often the ones most deeply tied to our relationship with self.

If you avoid rest, you may believe your worth is tied to output. If you avoid love, you may fear being seen. If you avoid money, you may carry shame or fear around power and control.

Avoidance is a mirror. It shows us the parts of ourselves we've disowned, denied or feared. But it also gives us a map. When we notice the pattern, we can trace it back, and begin to rewrite it.

 Reflection Prompts

- What area(s) of your *Balanced Success Wheel* do you consistently avoid?
- What emotions arise when you think about that area?
- Can you identify an earlier experience that might have influenced how you feel?
- What belief about yourself or the world is connected to that avoidance?

Rebuilding the Relationship

Awareness is the first step. Compassion is the second.

Start by gently reconnecting with the area you've avoided. Don't try to fix it all at once. Just notice. Bring curiosity instead of criticism. Choose one small action that moves you toward integration.

- If you've avoided finances, review one bank statement with neutrality.
- If you've ignored health, drink a glass of water and stretch.
- If you've buried your creative side, buy a notebook and write something for yourself.

Tiny steps are powerful. They say: "I'm ready to reclaim this part of myself."

Balanced Success Tool: The Avoidance Insight Map

Draw a table with three columns:

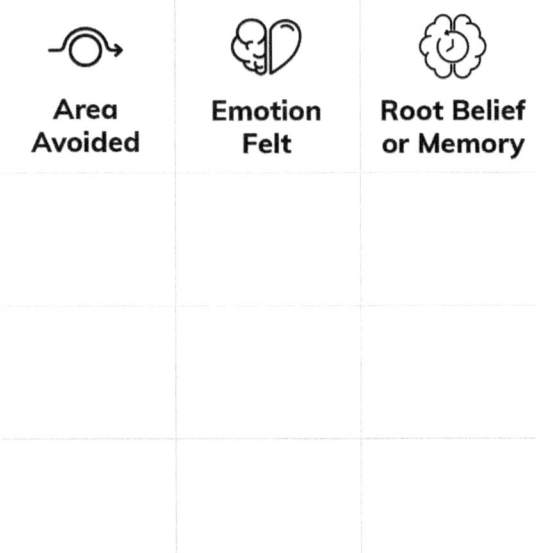

Area Avoided	Emotion Felt	Root Belief or Memory

Use this map to connect the dots. Understanding the story behind the avoidance gives you power. It moves you from shame to insight. From paralysis to choice.

Final Words

Neglect is not failure. It's feedback.

If there's a part of your life you've avoided, it's likely the part that needs the most love and attention. You are not broken for having blind spots. You are human. And now, you're becoming conscious.

The journey of *Balanced Success* is not about being perfect. It's about being whole. That includes the parts you've pushed away.

You are worthy of a life that includes all of you, even the parts you've been afraid to face.

It's time to stop digging and start listening.

 Key Messages: Taking Action

- Start with one clear next step.
- Put it in your calendar.
- Make it small enough to begin today.
- Prioritise consistency over intensity.
- Use habit stacking to build momentum.
- Design your environment to make the right action easy.
- Remove one blocker or distraction before you start.
- Track progress weekly in simple terms.
- Review, adjust, and keep moving.
- Ask for accountability and support.
- Celebrate small wins to lock in the behaviour.
- When you slip, reset at the next moment, not next Monday.

BALANCED SUCCESS

CHAPTER FOURTEEN

The Journey Ahead

Lead With Conscious Courage

And now, here we are. You've reached the final pages of this book, but in many ways, your journey is just beginning.

This book is a call to realign with your true self, return to what matters most and honour the essential foundations of a fulfilled and healthy life. In doing so, you'll become a resilient, grounded and inspiring leader; one who creates real change and empowers others through presence, not just performance.

It won't be easy. But as you already know, nothing truly worth it ever is. Endure the discomfort, face your fears and above all, build a relationship with yourself that is knowing, forgiving and understanding.

There is nothing more powerful than that.

Don't waste a minute. Lead like you never have before. Lead in a way that honours who you are and what truly matters.

Because only when you do that, do you create the space to lead through massive change, and to impact others in the most meaningful way possible.

Throughout these chapters, we've explored the real, raw and revealing layers of what it means to live a life of *Balanced Success*. Not just achievement. Not just wellness. But a fully integrated existence that honours true alignment.

We've spoken of clarity, of values, of vitality and habits, of finances and avoidance, of joy and pain, of rest and resilience. You've met the real me, through my wins, my wounds, my burnout and my breakthroughs. I didn't write this book to impress you. I wrote it to *connect* with you. To offer a hand across the table and say, *I've been there. And you don't have to stay stuck.*

And now, the world needs you awake.

We're living in a time of rapid acceleration. AI isn't just changing the workplace, it's changing what it means to be human. We are faced with unprecedented change, challenge and opportunity. In this landscape, leaders who remain disconnected, reactive or stuck in outdated paradigms will struggle. But leaders who are *aligned*, who know who they are, what they value, and how to stay grounded in chaos, will thrive.

The future isn't calling for more hustle. It's calling for more *humanity*.

> *"How we spend our days is, of course, how we spend our lives."* —
> **Annie Dillard,** *The Writing Life.*

Let that sink in.

Your calendar is your canvas; your choices are the brushstrokes. Make one intentional stroke today and let your future come into view.

This book was never about doing more.

It's about *being* more.

More present. More fulfilled. More aligned. More awake to the moments that make life rich, not just profitable.

A Final Invitation

So here is your invitation:

Choose to live wide awake. Choose to lead from a place of alignment. Choose to value *mental wealth* as highly as financial wealth. Choose to connect with those around you, and with yourself. Choose to become the kind of leader the future will thank you for.

And if you fall out of alignment (and you will), start again. That's the beautiful thing about this journey: it's yours. Every moment is a fresh opportunity to recalibrate.

Thank you for walking this path with me. Thank you for your courage, your curiosity and your willingness to grow.

The plane is ready. The flight plan is yours. It's time to lead, and live, with intention.

You are not here by accident. You are not broken. You are not behind. You are exactly where you need to be to begin again, on purpose, in power and with love.

With love and belief in you,

Tanya

For more information and resources visit: **alignedsuccess.com.au**

BALANCED SUCCESS

REFERENCES

Chapter One

Walker, T. (2024), *The Puppet Master's Bible: Pull the Hidden Strings of the Mind to Win Hearts and Open Wallets*, Tom Walker

Chapter Five

Blackburn, E. and Epel, E. (2017, 2025), *The Telomere Effect*, Grand Central Publishing

Van Dam, N. and van der Helm, E. (2016), *There's a Proven Link Between Effective Leadership and Getting Enough Sleep*, Harvard Business Review

National Institutes of Health. (2023). *Irregular sleep patterns linked with heart disease risks* (NHLBI news release, 1 March 2023). NHLBI, NIH

AdventHealth. (2023, Nov 20). *AdventHealth will lead $11 million national study on exercise and brain health.* AdventHealth

University of Sydney. (2023, Mar 2). *Poor sleep linked to years of poor cardiovascular health.* The University of Sydney

Pontzer, H. (2022). *Burn: The Misunderstood Science of Metabolism.* Penguin Press (AU ed.). Penguin

Inchauspé, J. (2022). *Glucose Revolution: The life-changing power of balancing your blood sugar.* Penguin Life.

Inchauspé, J. (2023). *The Glucose Goddess Method: Your four-week guide to cutting cravings, getting your energy back, and feeling amazing.* Penguin Life. Penguin

Solan, M. (2024, Jan 1). *How to lower your dementia risk.* Harvard Health Publishing. Harvard Health

Cheung, F. T. W., Li, X., Hui, T. K., Chan, N. Y., Chan, J. W. Y., Wing, Y. K., & Li, S. X. (2023). Circadian preference and mental health outcomes in youth: A systematic review and meta-analysis. *Sleep Medicine Reviews, 72,* 101851.

Burkart, Y. (Guest). (2024, Nov 18). *No.1 Toxicologist: Stop using scented candles! ...* (*The Diary of a CEO with Steven Bartlett* [Podcast]). Apple Podcasts.

United Nations Environment Programme (UNEP). (2023). *Chemicals in Plastics: A Technical Report.* (with contributions across WHO/UNEP plastics & health initiative context). Digital Library+1

Huberman, A. (2023). *Sleep Toolkit: Tools for optimizing sleep & sleep-wake timing* (Huberman Lab newsletter). Huberman Lab

JAMA Neurology (2024). *Effect of Sleep Restriction on Adolescent Cognition by Adiposity: A Randomized Crossover Trial.* JAMA Network

Zhang, J., Peng, M., Lian, E., Asimakopoulos, A. G., Luo, S., & Wang, L. (2023). Identification of poly(ethylene terephthalate) nanoplastics in commercially bottled drinking water using surface-enhanced Raman spectroscopy. *Environmental Science & Technology, 57*(21), 8365–8372.

Chapter Six

Prillenltensky, I. Institute for Mental Wealth, University of Birmingham, various

Brown, B. (2025), *Stop Being Too Friendly*, www.youtube.com

Clear, J. (2018, 2024), *Atomic Habits*, Avery Publishing

Chatterjee, R. (2019), *The Stress Solution*, Penguin Life

Brown, B. (2018), *Clear is Kind, Unclear is Unkind*, www.brenebrown.com

McKinsey (2025), *Make Faster, Better Decisions*, www.mckinsey.com

Harvard Business Review (2014), *Dear Diary*, www.hbr.org

Gallup (2024), *State of the Global Workplace Report*, www.gallup.com

Camp, A., Gast, A., Goldstein, D., & Weddle, B. (2024, February 12). *Organizational health is (still) the key to long-term performance.* McKinsey & Company.

Chapter Seven

Harvard University (1938 – present), *The Harvard Study of Adult Development,* www.adultdevelopmentstudy.org

Wang F. et al (2023), *A systematic review and meta-analysis of 90 cohort studies of social isolation, loneliness and mortality,* Nature Human Behaviour

Holt-Lunstad, J., Smith, T. B., & Layton, J. B. (2010). Social relationships and mortality risk: A meta-analytic review. *PLOS Medicine, 7*(7), e1000316.

Coutts, J. J., Al-Kire, R. L., & Weidler, D. J. (2023). I can see (myself) clearly now: Exploring the mediating role of self-concept clarity in the association between self-compassion and indicators of well-being. *PLOS ONE, 18*(6), e0286992.

Chapter Eight

Shanafelt, T. D. (2021). Physician well-being 2.0: Where are we and where are we going? *Mayo Clinic Proceedings, 96*(10), 2682–2693).

Dunbar, R. et al (2012), *Social laughter is correlated with an elevated pain threshold,* Proceedings of the Royal Society B

Chapter 10

Peter, S. et al (2024), *The 2025 Skills Horizon,* Sydney Executive Plus, The University of Sydney

Chapter 11

Csikszentmihalyi, M. (2022), *Flow, the Psychology of Happiness*, Penguin

Tummers, L. G., & Bakker, A. B. (2021). Leadership and Job Demands–Resources theory: A systematic review. *Frontiers in Psychology, 12*, 722080.

Yukl, G. (2012). Effective leadership behaviour: What we know and what we need to know. *Academy of Management Perspectives, 26*(4), 66–85.

Dispenza, J. (2012). *Breaking the habit of being yourself: How to lose your mind and create a new one.*

HeartMath Institute (2022), *Heart-brain coherence research*, www.heartmath.com

Chapter 13

Donaldson, S. I., van Zyl, L. E., & Donaldson, S. I. (2022). PERMA+4: A framework for work-related wellbeing, performance and Positive Organizational Psychology 2.0. *Frontiers in Psychology, 12*, 817244.

Blanchflower, D. G., & Oswald, A. J. (2011). International happiness: A new view on the measure of performance. *Academy of Management Perspectives, 25*(1), 6–23

www.ingramcontent.com/pod-product-compliance
Lightning Source LLC
Chambersburg PA
CBHW060355080526
44583CB00012B/322